GREAT GARNISHES 盤飾精選

黃淑惠 編著 Edited by Su-Huei Huang

味全食譜
Wei-Chuan Cookbook

編著：黃淑惠

作者：湯美凱利、江德全、何建忠、呂瑞義、吳銀宗、洪銀龍
連武德、陳兆麟、曹麗娟、張金聰、鄭衍基、劉榮枝、魏幸助

翻譯：賴燕貞

文稿協助：邱澄子、何久恩、馬優雅、陳素真、詹麗莎、黃穎新

照相：大野現

封面設計：王瑾

設計：張菲

味全出版社　版權所有：局版台業字第0179號

1990年5月初版
1997年2月5版　5-4-8
1998年6月修訂初版
2007年10月修訂6版

EDITOR: Su-Huei Huang
CONTRIBUTORS: Tomi Carey, Te-Chuan Chiang, Chien-Chung
Ho, Jui-I Lu, Yin-Tsung Wu, In-Long Hung, Wu-Te Lien, Choa-
Lin Chen, Li-Chuan Tsao, Chin-Tsung Chang, Yen-Chi Cheng,
Jung-Chin Liu, Shin-Chu Wei
TRANSLATOR: Yen-Jen Lai
EDITORIAL STAFF: Cheng-Tze Chiu, John Holt,
Gloria C. Martinez, Su-Jen Chen, Lisa Jan, Vincent Wong

PHOTOGRAPHY: Aki Ohno
COVER DESIGN: Chin Ong
DESIGN: F.S. Chang
PRINTED IN TAIWAN

WEI-CHUAN PUBLISHING
1455 Monterey Pass Rd., #110
Monterey Park, CA 91754, U.S.A.
Tel: (323)261-3880
Fax: (323)261-3299
www.weichuancookbook.com
wc@weichuancookbook.com

FIRST PRINTING: MAY 1990
5th PRINTING: FEBRUARY 1997
REVISED EDITION, FIRST PRINTING: JUNE 1998
REVISED EDITION, SIXTH PRINTING: OCTOBER 2007

ISBN-13: 978-0-941676-21-2
ISBN-10: 0-941676-21-8

序　自民國七十一年出版〝拼盤與盤飾〞一書以來，深受愛好切雕藝術的讀者歡迎，並來函要求出版更多有關拼盤或盤飾方面的書籍，本人因此深受鼓勵，為滿足愛好者的需要，乃決定由國內外各方面廣泛蒐集更多更完善的資料，以惠我讀者，因而走訪各地烹飪班、餐廳，並藉著味全文教基金會金廚獎的舉辦，取得國內多位頂尖盤飾切雕師傅的大力協助，並且由於美國的湯美凱利女士的參與，俾使得予彙集整理而完成本書〝盤飾精選〞。

本書〝盤飾精選〞與〝拼盤與盤飾〞最大的區別是加入了很多餐桌主題裝飾，全部使用蔬菜、水果及其他食物做成。依聚會的性質，如生日、情人節、萬聖節、聖誕節或各種大小型自助餐會，都可在書內找出適宜的餐桌主題來應用。

目錄的安排以師傅們的姓氏筆劃，依序排列出其所有作品，可突顯出各家各派的雕飾風格，讓讀者更能了解並欣賞切雕藝術。

本書能順利完成，除了特別要感謝台灣多位師傅及美國湯美凱利女士和其先生的協助外，對於味全文教基金會的襄助及現代製圖公司所提供的4張西方盤飾的底片，謹此致上萬分謝意。

Introduction

CHINESE APPETIZERS AND GARNISHES was first published in 1982. Responses from readers throughout the world indicate that it is the best garnish book they have ever seen. "It's too pretty to eat!" or "We eat with our eyes!" are comments often used to describe the garnishes in this book. It takes very little to present food beautifully and the rewards are most gratifying. Cookbook collectors treasure it! They have also requested that we continue to publish more garnish books. GREAT GARNISHES is Wei-Chuan's response to this demand.

GREAT GARNISHES is a compilation of prize-winning garnishes submitted by cooking schools, restaurants, and garnish master chefs in Taiwan who participated in contests sponsored by the Wei-Chuan Cultural Educational Foundation, with contributions from Tomi Carey of the United States of America.

The major difference between GREAT GARNISHES and CHINESE APPETIZERS AND GARNISHES is the centerpiece garnishes created from vegetables, fruits and other cooking materials, which are added in this book. With the rich contents in this book, readers can always find a suitable garnish centerpiece for any special event such as a birthday, Valentine's Day, Halloween, Christmas, banquet feast or gourmet buffet.

The Table of Contents lists the names of the garnish experts followed by the garnishes they prepared. This enables the reader to see, to enjoy, and to select from various styles.

I would like to acknowledge and express my appreciation to all who have contributed to this book. To the master chefs and Wei-Chuan Cultural Educational Foundation in Taiwan for the beautiful Chinese garnishes they provided. To Tomi Carey, for her contribution of the Western garnishes. To her husband, executive chef Johnny Carey, for preparing the food used in her presentations. Finally, I extend special gratitude to Modern Age Graphics for providing four negatives of the western garnishes.

Huang Su Hui

目 錄　CONTENTS

作者簡介 · CONTRIBUTORS

湯美凱利 不僅是食品專家，且是五本食譜的作者、烹飪老師、宴會籌備人、食品公司和經銷商顧問，烹飪比賽的裁判，同時也是廚師烹飪協會和國際烹飪協會的會員，並曾在多種特別場合演講。為增廣經驗及精進手藝，她曾遊歷超過40個國家。

湯美曾任報紙和雜誌的專欄作家。經常上電視接受訪問，並在洛杉磯的電台主持〝湯美深夜點心〞節目。她同時也是廚具進口商和加拿大〝凱利〞餐廳的所有人。

Tomi Carey's expertise extends beyond her reputation as a food expert. She is the author of five cookbooks, a cooking instructor, fine caterer, consultant and food advisor for cooking manufacturers as well as a guest lecturer for various special events. Tomi has also traveled in more than 40 countries to increase her knowledge of the cooking arts.

Tomi has been a columnist for many newspapers and magazines. She has made many guest appearances on television and had her own radio food talk show in Los Angeles, "A Late Night Snack with Tomi Ryan". She is a housewares importer, and the proprietor of "Carey's By The Sea" restaurant-resort in Bathurst, N.B. Canada.

江德全 台灣省宜蘭市人，韓香亭餐廳主廚，曾榮獲第2屆金饗獎第一名，金廚獎第4屆烹飪組優勝，第5屆蔬果雕刻創意獎，第7屆蔬果雕刻第一名，烹飪組創意獎及冰雕佳作，金手指冰雕大賽第三名。

Te-Chuan Chiang
Mr. Chiang served as a master chef at Han Shiang Ting Restaurant in Taipei. He won the Grand Prize in the Golden Banquet Contest and 3rd Prize in the Golden Finger Ice Carving Contest. Other prizes include Excellent Chef Award and Creativity Award in the Cooking Category, Grand Prize and Creativity Award in the Vegetable and Fruit Carving Category, and Best Performance Award in the Ice Carving Category in the Wei-Chuan Golden Chef Contest.

何建忠 台北市人，現任職國賓大飯店西餐部，曾榮獲1987年亞太切雕冠軍，蛋捲料理季軍，中華百家名廚冰雕冠軍，金廚獎第4屆及第6屆冷盤裝飾季軍，第7屆冰雕亞軍及冷盤裝飾優勝。

Chien-Chung Ho Mr. Ho has performed in the Ming Garden Dining Room of the Ambassador Hotel in Taipei. He won the Grand Prize in the Pacific Asia Carving Contest, 3rd Prize in the Egg Roll Cuisine Contest, and Grand Prize in the China Chef Ice Carving Contest. Other prizes include 3rd Prize and Excellent Chef Award in the Cold Plate Category, and 2nd Prize in the Ice Carving Category in the Wei-Chuan Golden Chef Contest.

呂瑞義 高雄市人，任職全省素食餐廳高雄店領班。

Jui-I Lu Mr. Lu is a native of Kaohsiung, Taiwan. He has worked as captain at the Chyuan Sheeng Vegetarian Restaurant in Kaohsiung.

吳銀宗 台灣省宜蘭市人，現任職山海關餐廳。曾榮獲65年基隆市黨部蔬果切雕比賽冠軍，金廚獎第7屆蔬果雕刻佳作，第8屆蔬果雕刻創意獎及職業組第一名。

Yin-Tsung Wu Mr. Wu has performed at the Shan Hai Kwan Restaurant. In 1976, he won the Grand Prize in the Vegetable and Fruit Carving Contest in Keelung. Other prizes include Best Performance Award and Creativity Chef Award in the Vegetable and Fruit Carving Category, and Grand Prize in the Restaurant Platter Category in the Wei-Chuan's Golden Chef Contest.

洪銀龍 台灣省南投縣人，味全家政班素食烹飪教師，現任法華素食餐廳董事長，行政院青輔會素食專任教師，中華民國烹飪協會會員，全國素食超市顧問，曾獲金廚獎4-8屆素食組優勝，佳作及創意獎。

In-Long Hung Mr. Hung is a former instructor of Wei-Chuan Vegetarian Cooking Classes, and director of Fa Hua Vegetarian Restaurant. An instructor of National Youth Commission of Executive Yuan, member of the China Cooking Association, and consultant of the Nation-wide Vegetarian Supermarket Co., Ltd. His awards include Excellent Chef Award, Best Performance Award, and Creativity Award in the Vegetarian Cooking Category in the Wei-Chuan Golden Chef Contest.

連武德 台灣省台北縣人，曾任職國聲酒店、海霸王及甲天下主廚，並獲1988年金廚獎蔬果雕刻第三名。

Wu-Te Lien Mr. Lien was the master chef at the Kuo Sheng Hotel, Hai Pa Wang and Jar Ten Shah restaurants. He has won 3rd Prize in the Vegetable and Fruit Carving Category in the Wei-Chuan Golden Chef Contest.

陳兆麟 台灣省宜蘭縣人，曾榮獲第6屆金廚獎職業組蔬果雕刻優勝，第8屆職業組蔬果雕刻亞軍及職業組烹飪優勝，第2屆飲食工會舉辦之烹飪季軍，現任職渡小月食堂。

Choa-Lin Chen
Prizes Mr. Chen has won include 2nd Prize and excellent Chef Award in the Vegetable and Fruit Carving Category and Excellent Chef Award in the Restaurant Platter Cooking Category in Wei-Chuan Golden Chef Contest. He has also won 3rd Prize in the Cooking Contest held by the Food Union. Mr. Chen performs at the Do Hsiao Yuoh Restaurant.

曹麗娟 台北市人，現任伊比國際產品包裝設計公司負責人，曾榮獲金廚獎第5屆職業組冷盤裝飾創意獎，第8屆業餘組全國第一名。

Li-Chuan Tsao Ms. Tsao served as director of a packaging-design company. She has won the Creativity Award in the Restaurant Cold Plate Category and Grand Prize in the Amateur Cold Plate Category in the Wei-Chuan Golden Chef Contest.

張金聰 台灣省彰化縣人，現任職康華大飯店及北安國中中菜烹飪班教師。

Chin-Tsung Chang Mr. Chang has cooked at the Golden China Hotel and has served as cooking instructor in Pei-Ann Girl's Junior High School.

鄭衍基 福建省福州市人，任教於實踐家專及文化大學家政系海青班，現任職國賓大飯店，曾榮獲金饗獎梅花烹飪比賽職業甲組第二名，亞太地區海鮮烹調冠軍，蔬果切雕季軍，78年觀光局主辦之蔬果切雕佳作等。

Yen-Chi Cheng Mr. Cheng worked at Shin Chien Home Economics College and taught a Technique Training Class for Overseas Youth for the Department of Home Economics, Chinese Culture University. He also cooked at the Ambassador Hotel in Taipei. His prizes include 2nd Prize in the Restaurant Platter Cooking Category in the Wei-Chuan Golden Banquet Contest, Grand Prize in the Seafood Cooking Contest, 3rd Prize in the Vegetable and Fruit Carving Contest in Asia Pacific, and Best Performance Award in the Vegetable and Fruit Carving Contest held by the Tourism Bureau.

劉榮枝 台灣省新竹縣人，現任來來喜來登大飯店雕花師，曾獲第7屆金廚雕花創意獎及第8屆金廚雕花優勝獎。

Jung-Chih Liu Mr. Liu has worked as a carving chef in Lai Lai Sheraton Hotel. He has won the Creativity Award and Excellent Chef Award in the Carving Category in the Wei-Chuan Golden Chef Contest.

魏幸助 台灣省宜蘭市人，現任環亞飯店滿漢宮雕花師，曾榮獲第5屆金廚獎蔬果雕刻第三名，第6屆第二名，第7屆優勝及第8屆佳作及創意獎。

Shin-Chu Wei Mr. Wei is the carving chef in Man Han Palace Dining Room in the Asia World Plaza Hotel in Taipei. He has won 2nd and 3rd Prizes, Excellent Chef Award, Best Performance Award, and Creativity Award in the Vegetable and Fruit Carving Category in the Wei-Chuan Golden Chef Contest.

盤飾需知及工具 · GARNISHING TIPS AND TOOLS

製作精緻、出色的盤飾除仰賴純熟的技巧及經驗外，以下盤飾需知及工具可使盤飾的製作更為成功及容易。

儲存：切雕好的盤飾（除番茄、西瓜之類外），可依蔬菜類別，分別泡在有水的乾淨容器內，或用濕巾包好，放入塑膠袋內置冰箱冷藏，可以維持新鮮一星期左右。

食物膠：如欲防止食物變色，或想將不同盤飾黏在一起，可利用食物膠（見41頁吉利膠）。

染色：染色時可將食用色素放入容器內，加水調成需要的顏色，盤飾泡的時間越長，顏色越深。

Delicate and outstanding garnishes rely on experience and technique. The following garnishing tips and tools can make your garnishes more successful and easier to create.

Storage: Garnishes, except tomato and melon, will keep fresh for a week, if they are sorted and stored in clean water in covered containers; or covered with wet paper towels then wrapped in a plastic bag, and refrigerated.

Food Glue (Gelatin Glue): Useful for holding together such garnishes as the Apple Bird (p. 41) and Cantaloupe Vase (p. 40) and will also prevent discoloration.

Coloring the Garnishes: Put food coloring into a plastic bag. Add water to get the desired color shade. Put the garnish to be colored in the bag. The color will take immediately and will set in a few minutes. The longer the garnish soaks in the coloring, the richer the color will be.

花模
不同形狀及大小的花模，可用來壓花。

Cutters
There are different cutter sizes and shapes which can be used to create designs easily.

沙拉器
將紅、白蘿蔔、黃瓜、馬鈴薯或甜菜等蔬菜放入機器內，轉動把手即可切出長絲或花朵。

Saladacco
Instant flowers and long shreds can be made by inserting vegetables, such as carrots, cucumbers, radishes, potatoes, beets, turnips, etc. into the Saladacco, and turning the handle.

薄菜刀
舉凡切塊、切片等均使用薄菜刀。

Thin-blade Cleaver
The thin-blade cleaver is used to slice and cut material into sections.

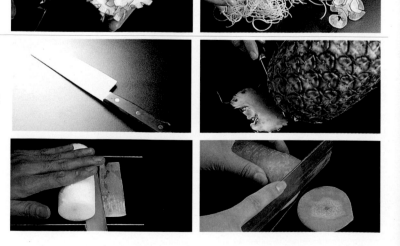

尖刀

用來雕較細膩的部份，例如雕花瓣、片薄片、薄皮、刻圖案。。

Sharp-pointed Knife

The sharp-pointed knife is used to make fine and delicate cuts, such as carving petals, slicing the skin off vegetables, or engraving designs.

剪刀

剪刀的用途很廣，除剪綠葉、花瓣外，也用來剪蝦頭、牙籤等。

Scissors

Scissors are very useful. Besides cutting leaves and petals, they may also be used to cut off shrimp heads and toothpicks.

雕花刀

大、中、小三支成套，一端尖形，另一端圓形。尖形一端可用來雕尖形花瓣、劃線、刻鋸齒紋。圓形一端可用來雕圓形花瓣或挖圓孔。雕花刀本公司有售。

Carving Tools

Three different sizes of tools in a set; each tool has both a v-shaped-blade and a curved-blade. The v-shaped-blade carving tool is used to make pointed petals, v-shaped grooves, and strips. The curved-blade carving tool is used to make the scallop petals, and to cut holes. Carving tools are available from Wei-Chuan Publishing.

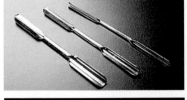

裝飾雕刀

有尖形和圓形雕刀，由於尺寸較上面雕花刀大，故除以上用法外，尚適用於較大型的水果，且可去果核和挖黃瓜。

Deco Knives

The deco knives are available in "v" shape and "u" shape and are larger than carving tools. Besides the functions outlined for carving tools, the deco knives may also be used for carving larger fruits, coring apples, and scooping out cucumbers.

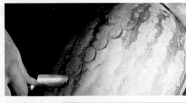

心

將綠葉和各種不同的花用牙籤插在心形的保麗龍上即成美麗的心。

蘋果鳥做法參考第41頁。

番紅花做法參考第23頁。

小紅蘿蔔菊花做法參考第11頁。

法國玫瑰做法參考第35頁。

蒜菊花做法參考第32頁。

洋菇花做法參考第27頁。

聖誕紅做法參考第33頁。

半球形圓頂花做法參考第25頁。

其他花的做法亦包含在此書內，讀者可自行選擇喜歡的花來做此心。

Heart

The heart is made with a rigid polystyrene plastic, covered with greenery and flowers that are secured with toothpicks. Instructions for the details may be found on the following pages:

All the other flowers are also included in this book. Create other centerpieces by selecting flowers of your choice.

垂直扇和水平扇

長形的小紅蘿蔔直或橫放，垂直縱切即可做成紅白相間的垂直扇及水平扇。此盤飾簡單易做，短時間内即可完成。

1 選擇長形的小紅蘿蔔，切除根莖二端。

2 由根向莖垂直縱切數刀，不切斷。

3 另一邊如上法再垂直切數刀。泡水使扇張開成垂直扇。

4 亦可將蘿蔔橫放，由根端向莖端連續垂直切相連薄片，即成水平扇。

● 包心菜置容器上，四週插上各式各樣的花，即成一盆美麗的盆景。

Vertical and Horizontal Fan

Simple and straight cuts on a long radish produce beautiful red-and-white vertical and horizontal fans which are especially useful when time is limited.

1 Use a long radish, cut off the root without cutting into the radish. Cut off greenery, leaving 1/8" (0.3cm).

2 Make several deep, vertical cuts from root end toward stem, do not cut through.

3 Repeat same cuts on the opposite side. Soak in water until garnish opens to form vertical fan.

4 A horizontal fan is made in the same manner, but lay it horizontally.

● Different kinds of flowers may be inserted using toothpicks around a cabbage to make a beautiful flower pot.

小 紅 蘿 蔔 盤 飾 · RADISH GARNISH

菊花

簡單的垂直切法應用在長形的小紅蘿蔔上，即可做出漂亮且看似複雜的花。

1 由根向莖垂直縱切數刀至中央。

2 另一邊，同上法切數刀至中央。

3 另一個方向，再垂直縱切數刀成十字形。

4 繼續垂直縱切，至全部切完。泡水使用。

Chrysanthemum

A very beautiful and complicated appearing flower is made by using simple straight cuts on a long radish.

1 Make several deep, vertical cuts from the root end toward the stem. Do not cut through.

2 Repeat the same cuts on the opposite side.

3 Continue the same procedures on the third side; these cuts should cross the cuts in steps *1* and *2*.

4 Continue to cut the fourth side while holding the radish together with fingertips. It will bloom in cold water.

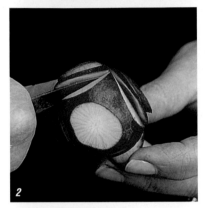

祖母玫瑰

這種小紅蘿蔔玫瑰看似骰子，但由於一般祖母輩常在特殊場合採用，故又稱祖母玫瑰。

1　由根部切掉一塊，露出白色圓形，再由四邊直切四片花瓣。

2　亦可再刻一層花瓣。

3　花瓣邊緣用剪刀剪成鋸齒狀以添趣味。

4　內部白肉可修成圓錐形加以應用，此法尤其適用於有缺陷的小紅蘿蔔。

Grandmother's Rose

This is the popular radish rose that grandmother likes to make for special occasions.

1　Cut off the radish root to expose a white circle. Cut a petal on each of all four sides, leaving a red margin between each petal and the top.

2　To be more creative, cut row of petals behind each of the first layer.

3　Interest may be heightened to the simple rose by cutting small "V 's" on the petals with a scissors to give a fringed look.

4　In the case of blemished or poorly shaped radishes, trim the inside to form a cone.

小 紅 蘿 蔔 盤 飾 · R A D I S H   G A R N I S H E S

棒棒糖

此種楔形片切法可應用來做車輪、拐杖糖、汽球或日本燈籠。

1 由莖向根，切下楔形片（切二斜刀，成 "V" 形，相交於中央）。

2 同上法整圈切完即成。

3 亦可將蒜葉、包心菜或其它有葉的蔬菜剪成葉形。

4 或以梗為中心，將葉對折後剪細長條，再打開沿梗剪成二半即成羊齒葉，可應用在盤飾上。

Candy Cane

The "V" or wedge cut is used to create a candy cane, pin wheel, balloon, or Japanese lantern effect.

1 Cut a vertical wedge from the side of a radish taking care not to cut into the bottom or top ends.

2 Continue to do a series of these cuts around the radish. The shape of radish will determine its appearance.

3 Create leaves by cutting leeks, cabbages or other leafy vegetables into desired shapes with a scissors.

4 Create a fern leaf by cutting narrow strips along folded leek leaves; cut almost to the center. Cut the leaf lengthwise in half through the center vein. Place in cold water, it will curl in an hour.

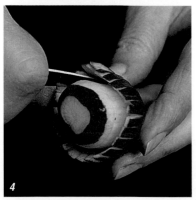

簡易雛菊

使用蘋果切片器可在短時間內做出美麗的花。

1 將小紅蘿蔔放在布上，以避免切時滑動。

2 可去除花心，以便裝沾料或沙拉。

3 若無切片器則由小紅蘿蔔上方劃一圓圈做為花瓣頂端的基準線，由此基準線至底部直切出一圈花瓣。

4 用小尖刀沿著花瓣深切一圈，也可挖除一圈餘肉使花瓣張開，泡水使用。

Short Cut Daisy

An apple slicer provides both speed and beauty.

1 Place the radish on a cloth to keep it from rolling and to prevent cutting off the petals from cutting too deep.

2 Remove the center if you wish to fill the radish with a dip for salad.

3 A hand-made daisy requires a round radish. Cut a white circle on the top; cut another circle below it which becomes the guideline for the petal tops. Make vertical cuts from the second line to the radish bottom to create petals.

4 Insert the knife tip behind the petals to free them from the radish. Place the flower in water to bloom.

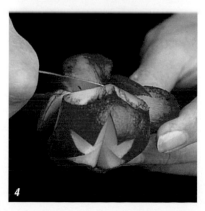

星形花

頂部的星形用楔形片（"V"形）切法。花瓣則切成上薄下厚的花瓣。

1 在頂部以二個斜刀切下楔形片（切二斜刀，成"V"形，相交於中央）。同法切下第二片，使頂端成"X"形。

2 同上法再切下第三片，頂端成星形。

3 用小刀的尖端沿圓周面刻出花瓣，花瓣上薄下厚。

4 花瓣要相連。

Star Flower

The "V" or wedge cut is used to make the star and the "(" or curve cut is used to make graceful petals. The petals are very thin at the top and thick at the bottom for realism.

1 Remove a narrow wedge from the top of the radish. Repeat the same size wedge to form an "X".

2 Remove a third wedge directly across the "X" to form a six-pointed star.

3 Form petals by using the knife tip, following the contour of the radish. Flower petals are cut thin at the top, rounded and thicker at the base.

4 Petals are adjoining; no red strips in between them.

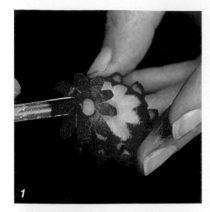

雕花刀應用

雕花刀（參考第7頁）易操作，可在短時間內做出美麗的花朵。

1　花瓣可雕一層或數層。雕刀用尖形或圓形均隨意。

2　將小紅蘿蔔底部翻過來雕一圈花瓣。插入雕刀時，由薄逐漸向莖部的中央增厚。雕時每一刀必須深入莖部中央，挑除整圈花瓣時才不會破裂。

3　也可挖出花心，填入不同的顏色。

●　雕好的花可插在藍內與其他盤飾一起陳列，形成美麗的花藍。

Tool Tricks

Carving tools (See p. 7) create instant "no fail" flowers with "oval" or "pointed" petals.

1　Use a v-shaped blade or curve-shaped blade carving tool, carve as many rows of petals as desired.

2　Turn radish over; make a flower shape on top by starting the cut 1/4 of the way down the radish stem. Start very thin and thicken the petal as the tool enters into the center of the radish. All cuts must meet in the center of the radish for the flower shape to come off in one piece.

3　Create interest on top by taking the core out of the radish and replacing it with a core from another vegetable.

●　Carved flowers may be arranged in a basket or displayed with other garnishes.

小紅蘿蔔盤飾 · RADISH GARNISHES

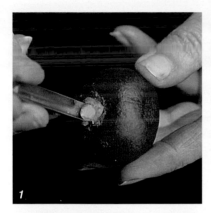

小紅蘿蔔洋菇

表面有瑕疵的小紅蘿蔔，不必丟棄，可利用來雕此有趣的迷你小洋菇。

1 沿莖刻小圓圈，莖不挖掉。
2 雕一圈花瓣成小菊花狀。
3 在小菊花下方，刻一圓圈，小心不要切斷。
4 由小紅蘿蔔的另一端向莖部切除多餘的部份，使成洋菇的柄。

Mushroom-shaped Radish

Create intriguing miniature mushrooms for greater interest. This is an ideal garnish to make when radishes are cracked or imperfect since that portion will be peeled away.

1 Use a small carving tool to cut a circle around the green end of a radish. Leave the green intact.
2 Remove the red skin only to create a white daisy.
3 To make mushroom cap, cut under the daisy being careful not to slice off the cap; leave room for the mushroom stem.
4 Create the stem by slicing the radish from the bottom up to the cap.

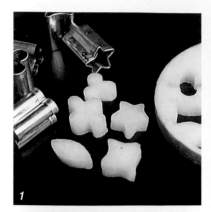

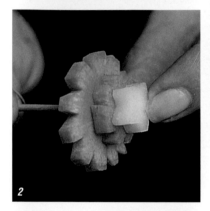

雛菊

小花簡單易做，可應用在每日的日常生活中，如加入湯、沙拉內或用來拌炒或做點心。

1 用小花模壓花心。

2 紅、白蘿蔔粗細各一段在圓周面刻數條 "V" 形直溝後切片，再用牙籤將三種不同大小片串成菊花。

3 葡萄柚或包心菜上蓋綠葉蔬菜後，插上菊花固定。

4 中央先插一朵菊花，再對稱插四週，花朵數目可隨意。

Daisies

These carrot flowers are so easy to make they can be used in every meal every day; in soups, salads, stir-fries, and snacks.

1 Use small cutters to create flower centers.

2 Cut 2 sections of carrot of different thicknesses. Cut long V-shaped strips lengthwise around the carrot sections then slice it. Insert tooth-picks into 3 different sized slices to make the daisies.

3 Cover a grapefruit or a cabbage with firm greenery like kale. Secure and decorate it with daisies.

4 Balance the arrangement by starting with a center flower and placing equal numbers of flowers on each side.

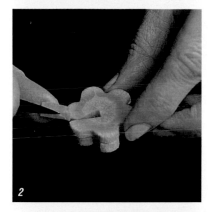

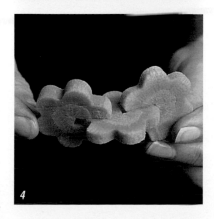

花

二片紅蘿蔔互相插入所做成的花，令人有整朵花雕出的錯覺。

1. 紅蘿蔔切成0.5公分厚片，用花模壓成花狀。
2. 二片紅蘿蔔花重疊。用小尖刀由中心向旁邊切除一片。缺口中央寬，外窄；中央寬度應和紅蘿蔔片厚度一樣。
3. 由缺口處，將二片紅蘿蔔互相插入。
4. 許多片串連即成鏈條狀。亦可採用不同顏色的蔬菜以造成特殊效果。

Jacks

Flower made by sliding two pieces together which fit so well that it looks like one piece made by carving.

1. Cut the carrot into slices about 1/4" (0.5cm) thick. Use a cutter to create a flower from the slices.
2. Sandwich two slices together. Place the point of a knife just past center. Cut through both sides and remove a wedge, as illustrated. The widest part of the notch must be the same as the thickness of one slice. The outside end of the notch is slightly narrower because the tension of the carrot is released when cutting and it will spring open slightly.
3. Slide the two pieces together, fitting a carrot slice into the notch. It should fit firmly so it looks like one piece.
4. An interesting chain is created by linking many carrot slices together. Different color vegetables can be combined to add an unusual effect.

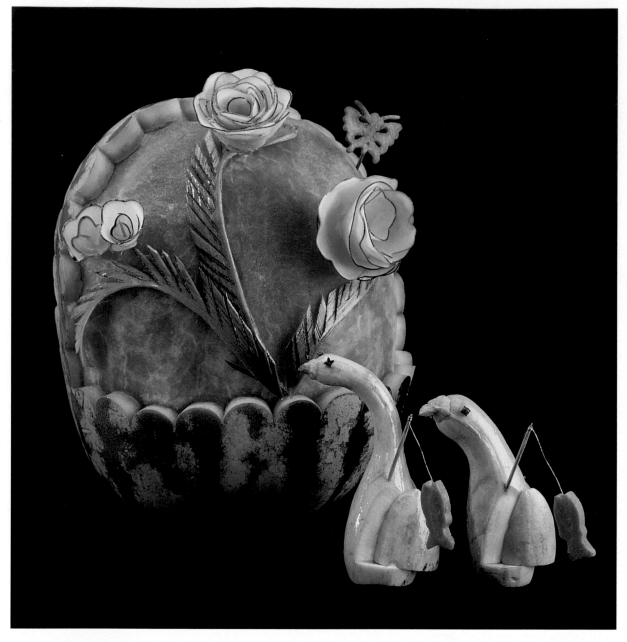

西瓜籃與漁夫

西瓜籃做法參考第52頁的水救籃，鴨子做法參考第21頁，小花做法參考第6頁沙拉器。

Melon Basket and Fisherman

Instructions for the details may be found on the following pages. Melon Basket, page 52, Duck, page 21, Squash flowers, page 6 (Saladacco)

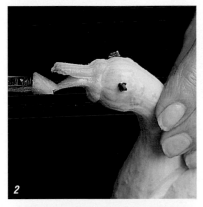

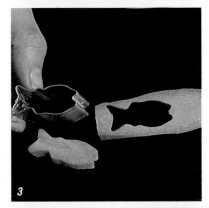

鴨子釣魚

選擇脖子圓而彎曲，較有特徵而大小不同的瓜類。

1 兩邊各直切一刀至離底部1公分處止。再各橫切一刀使翅膀可移動。

2 插入丁香粒做為眼睛。莖部切開或切一片紅蘿蔔用牙籤插入做為嘴巴。

3 紅蘿蔔斜切片，再用花模壓成魚。

4 取細鐵絲一端綁在牙籤上，另一端穿入魚嘴做為釣魚線。再將牙籤插在鴨身上即成。

Fishing Duck

Select curved-neck squashes that have the character of a nice round neck; different sizes can create a duck family.

1 On each side of the squash, slice down to 1/2" (1cm) from the bottom. Cut across that line to provide a shelf for the wings; slide wings back for a proper effect.

2 Insert cloves for eyes. Cut an open beak on stem or cut a piece of a carrot for a beak and hold it in place with a toothpick.

3 Cut carrot into diagonal slices to provide more surface to cut a fish.

4 Wire from a bag tie is twisted onto a toothpick. Insert the other end of the wire into the fish's mouth to create a fishing pole.

扇形鵝

選用黃瓜、意大利瓜或彎脖子的瓜類切成扇形，再加上眼睛和腳，即成有趣的鵝。

1 瓜縱切兩半。頸部以下用楔形片切法（切二斜刀，成 "V" 形，相交於中央）切橫溝。

2 由頸部以下直切薄片，用手輕壓使薄片張開成扇形。

3 鑲入丁香粒為鵝眼。紅蘿蔔做鵝腳。

4 也可將底部橫切除一片，再由頸部以下直切薄片成圍裙，將鵝直立，脖子套上紅蘿蔔環即成 "玻里尼西亞舞者"。

Fan Goose

A simple fan can be cut from a curved-neck squash, a cucumber, or a zucchini. Add more interest by placing eyes and feet.

1 Cut the squash lengthwise in half. Cut and remove narrow wedges across the squash.

2 Leave the narrow "neck" intact. Cut lengthwise slices. Gently press the top of slices to spread them into fan.

3 Insert a clove for an eye and create the feet from a carrot slice.

4 The "Polynesian Dancer" is created by cutting off a slice from the bottom then cutting vertical slices through the whole squash base to make the skirt. The lei is cut from a carrot; use cloves for the eyes.

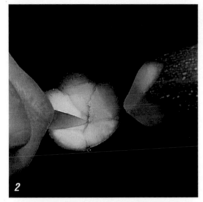

番紅花

番紅花可利用紅蘿蔔、茄子、黃色瓜類或意大利瓜等材料。此花可生食,蒸熟或填塞食物食用。

1 手握刀身的中央,向瓜的底部切花瓣至約2/3處並迴轉半圈成一片花瓣。

2 步驟 *1* 內每一刀皆須在花中心相交,才能保持番紅花的完整而不破裂。

3 用堅實的蔬菜放在花的上、下二端,用牙籤串起固定,以做其它用途。

4 可配合花的顏色,選擇時令的蔬菜做為花心。

Crocus

This useful and attractive flower can be done on a carrot, a Japanese eggplant, a yellow squash as well as a zucchini. The flowers can be served raw, steamed, or stuffed.

1 Hold the knife in the middle of the blade. Starting toward the bottom, cut petals on an angle about 2/3 of the way into the zucchini. Turn the knife so that the tip of the blade ends in the center of the flower and the handle is parallel to the zucchini.

2 All cuts must meet in the center of the flower to enable the crocus to come off in one piece.

3 Secure the flower with a toothpick with firm vegetables on both sides of the crocus.

4 Create flower centers to suit color scheme and availability of produce.

瓜 類 盤 飾 · ZUCCHINI GARNISH

旋轉輪

此迷人的切法，不僅可增加意大利瓜的趣味，且適用於其它的瓜類。

1 意大利瓜片由中心直切一刀至厚度的3/4處止。

2 小刀由45°角再斜切一刀與第一刀相交，去除"V"形切片。

3 重覆作法1、2直至整圈切完。

4 任何堅實的蔬菜用模形壓成小花，放在瓜的上、下二端，用牙籤串起固定。

Pin Wheel

This fascinating cut adds interest not only to a zucchini but to melons as well.

1 Make a straight cut that is three quarters deep of the thickness of a slice of a zucchini.

2 Diagonally make a cut at a 45° angle, reaching the first cut. Remove the wedge created.

3 Repeat steps 1 and 2 until the row is completed.

4 Any piece of firm vegetable may be placed on a toothpick, then layered with a zucchini slice, followed by a firm center on top to be held in a floral arrangement.

半球形圓頂花

紅蘿蔔、白蘿蔔、甜菜類、馬鈴薯，甚至西瓜，都可應用此技巧，做成半球形圓頂花。工具的使用沒有限制，讀者可依自己的創意自行設計。

1 意大利瓜的頂部雕一圈花瓣，插入雕刀時由薄逐漸向莖部的中央增厚。雕時每一刀必須深入莖部中央，挑除整圈花瓣時才不會破裂。

2 刻二個相對的V成菱形，整圈刻完。

3 交替再刻數圈菱形。

4 去除瓜的頂部核心，代以紅蘿蔔。

● 盤內的紅蘿蔔是用沙拉器（參考第6頁）做成。

Floral Dome

The technique of making this dome can be used on carrots, turnips, beets, potatoes, and even melons. Special tools are helpful but not necessary in carving this design; create your own designs.

1 With the small carving tool, carve a daisy on top of the zucchini by starting the cut near the stem end of the zucchini. Start very thin and thicken the petal as the tool enters into the center of the zucchini. All cuts must meet in the center for the flower shape to come off in one piece.

2 Insert the medium carving tool, with the opening downward (V), into the green surface. One "V" cut and one "V" cut will make a diamond.

3 The remaining rows are formed by alternating diamonds.

4 Insert the small carving tool into the top center of the daisy to remove the core. Replace it with a core taken from a carrot.

● Carrot flowers in photo are done with a Saladacco (See p.6).

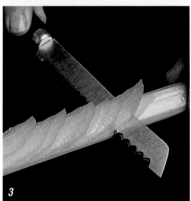

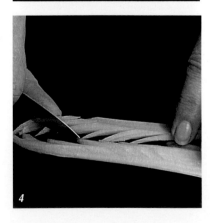

扇子和蕁蔴

切好的芹菜扇子不僅可用做盤飾，且可當做杓子來裝食物。蕁蔴的芹菜細條可直接生食，相當方便。

1　芹菜切段。沿莖的紋路，由較寬邊向窄邊直切細條成扇狀。

2　有綠葉部份，可將莖分開。泡水一天後即捲曲。

3　取芹菜莖，空心面向下。刀子20°角斜切片，不要切斷。

4　莖直切兩半，泡水一天以上即成蕁蔴。

Fan and Nettle

Cut celery functions as more than a garnish, it can also serve as a nice scoop for picking up dip. The nettle makes eating celery more pleasurable because the strings are cut.

1　Cut off the desired length for fans. Following the ribs, cut straight lines from the wide end to the narrow end of the stalk.

2　The leafy portion is used by splitting the stalk into several strips which will curl up after a day in water.

3　To make nettle, place the hollow side of stalk downward. Make close together crosswise slashes at a 20° angle along the back of the stalk, taking care not to cut through.

4　Cut stalk in half lengthwise. It will bloom after soaking in water for one or more days.

洋菇狂熱

雕花的洋菇可整顆加入湯、沙拉和燉的料理內使用;也可僅做為盤飾,效果都不錯。

1 用剝皮刀或尖頭雕刀由洋菇中心向外刻一圈月形溝。

2 小尖刀在洋菇中心壓星形,此壓紋顏色很快變黑,就可以顯出形狀。

3 如作法 **2**,壓星形,刻出另一種洋菇花。

4 食指放在洋菇下方,沿著星形外圍用小尖刀口壓一圈花紋。可任意安排花紋成喜歡的式樣。

Mushroom Manla

A decorated mushroom will get wonderful responses when used whole in soups, salads, stews or as a garnish.

1 Use a stripper or curved blade carving tool to cut lightly backward "('s" just through the skin of a mushroom.

2 Press the flat side of a pointed knife into the mushroom to create a star These Indentations will darken in minutes to show the design.

3 For another style, hold mushroom as shown and repeat directions in step **2**.

4 Hold index finger under the mushroom for support while depressing the tip of the knife toward the star to complete the design.

番茄盤飾 · TOMATO GARNISH

鬱金香

此簡單巧妙的盤飾可與食物一起食用。

1 選擇紅且硬的番茄切半後,再平行切四刀,至距底部1公分處止,不要切斷。

2 除最上面一片外,其餘切半。

3 略壓後,修整使張開成鬱金香。

4 用蔥做花梗,再將綠蔥一段,對角斜切成葉子。

Tomato Tulip

This simple and clever garnish can be included as part of the meal.

1 Select a firm red tomato; slice in half. Make 4 cuts parallel to the first cut to within 1/2" (1cm) of the blossom end.

2 Slice all but the top slice in half to the bud end.

3 Place light pressure on top of the tomato and arrange slices to open up like a tulip.

4 Use a green onion for the stem of the flower. Diagonally cut another green onion to form the leaves.

包 心 菜 盤 飾 · CABBAGE GARNISH

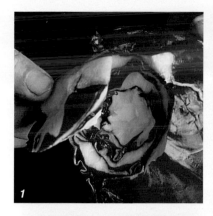

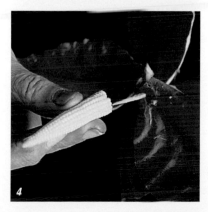

鳶尾花

紅色包心菜和蔥作成的鳶尾花不僅簡單、經濟、美麗，且可食用。

1 切除根部。

2 剝下菜葉，修剪成花瓣。

3 蔥內插入竹籤。

4 插入剪好的花瓣。三片朝上，三片朝下，中心用小玉米固定。如有必要，可使用數根牙籤固定花。

Iris

Imagine a flower arrangement of irises made from red cabbage and green onions only. It is easy, economical, stunning, and edible.

1 Cut off the root end around the core of the cabbage.

2 Peel off the leaves; trim leaves to resemble iris petals.

3 Cut off tip of green onion and insert a skewer in the end.

4 Place 3 petals facing down and 3 petals facing up to make an iris. The center may be a baby corn or the green onion root. More toothpicks may be used as needed to secure the flower.

洋 蔥 盤 飾 · ONION GARNISH

洋蔥燭台

此別緻且摔不破的燭台，由於使用前先放置冰箱內一、二天，故不會有辛辣味，而令人流淚。

1 在特大號的洋蔥頂上，切出星星的形狀。

2 挖出洋蔥的中心，大小恰可容納蠟燭。

3 由星星的尖端往下切至洋蔥底部1公分處止成寬花瓣。每一花瓣再切半也至底部1公分處止。

4 由外逐層打開花瓣，越外層張開愈大，像一朵花。燭台裝入塑膠袋內，置冰箱一、二天後使用。

Onion Candle Holder

There will be no tears when using this creative and unbreakable candle holder after it has been refrigerated for a day or two.

1 Cut a star pattern into the top of a very large onion.

2 Scoop out the center of the onion to allow the placement of a candle.

3 Cut petals starting from the points of the star to 1/2" (1cm) from the bottom. Cut these petals in two, to 1/2" (1cm) from the bottom of the onion.

4 When opening onion, it is important that only one row be opened at a time. Each row is pulled less outward than the previous row to look like a flower. Put the candle holder in a plastic bag then refrigerate it for a day or two.

洋蔥盤飾 · ONION GARNISH

荷花

洋蔥的大小形狀不一致，可自行創造變化花的型式。

1 先切除根部一片。

2 沿圓周深切5至8片花瓣，剝開成二半。

3 剝下外圍二圈，平放做為外圍花瓣。

4 剩餘的洋蔥，每一層略移動，使花瓣與花瓣層層交錯，放在外圍花瓣內，即成荷花。

Waterlily

Each onion has its own character, so do not be afraid to adapt these instructions as necessary. Create variations and flower styles.

1 Cut off the root end of the onion to release the layers.

2 Cut through to the middle of onion, as shown, to make five to eight petals depending on the size of onion. Pull the onion apart.

3 Remove outer two layers of the onion. Split rings and lay them flat to make the outer row.

4 Open up the remaining layers as desired; place them on the outside rows to make a waterlily.

蒜盤飾 · LEEK GARNISH

菊花

蔥或大洋蔥均可用來做此種菊花，染色後會有更好的特殊效果。

1 切除根部，但不要切到莖葉以免散開。用小尖刀在莖葉中段切 "∧" 形。

2 取根部直切成四等分，至距根1公分處止。

3 每一等分，由根部向頂部切半後再切半。僅切外面數層，中心處莖葉細，不必切到。

4 泡水數分鐘展開即可。浸泡水中可保持一星期不壞。

5 最外圈花瓣可用來裝食物或放入不同的花加以應用。

Mums (Chrysanthemum)

Green onion brushes and regular large onions are used to make this colorful mum. Color onions for a more stunning effect.

1 Cut off the root without cutting into the leek. Cut off desired length from middle of leek with a "∧" so petals will have pointed ends.

2 Cut the leek into four equal parts up to 1/2" (1cm) from the root end.

3 Split each quarter in half, then in half again. Starting from the root end through to the top of flower, cut through outer layers only.

4 Dip leek a few minutes in water then it is ready for use and can last a week if stored in water.

5 The outer rings can be used as food holders or insert different centers to create individual flowers.

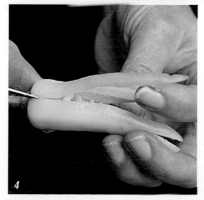

聖誕紅

紅椒或黃椒剪成聖誕紅形狀，適用於聖誕節。

1. 沿紅椒外圍剪一圈鋸形花瓣，剝開成為二朵花。
2. 剪開皮肉與種子接連處，使花瓣浸泡在水中時易於展開。
3. 如欲填塞食物，則將內部種子挖除。
4. 也可利用小辣椒，因大小形狀不同，做出來後有不同效果。

Poinsettias

Red and yellow peppers can be cut into poinsettias for Yuletide.

1. To cut petals, cut "up" between the ribs and "down" in the ribs. Divide the pepper in half.
2. Detach the rib membranes from the pepper and the seeds to allow petals to open in water.
3. Remove seeds only when desired or to fill it with food or dip.
4. Use differently sized small chili peppers to create exciting contrasts.

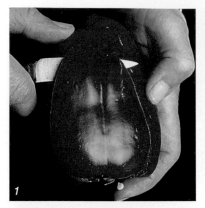

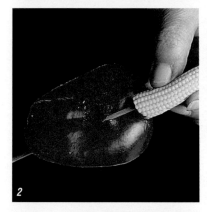

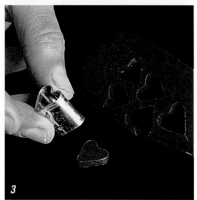

紅掌花

在芹菜上配以紅椒作成的紅掌花，有熱帶風味，奪人眼目。

1 一個紅椒可作三或四朵花，紅椒脊部應在花的中間。

2 將竹籤穿過紅椒並插入小玉米或雕過的蘿蔔即成紅掌花。

3 用小花模將紅椒或紅蘿蔔等壓成小花，可用來當裝飾。

4 芹菜莖上塗一些奶油起司或其他填料，即成精美的開胃小菜。

Anthurium

Anthuriums not only add a tropical touch, but also provide eye-catching color.

1 Three or four anthuriums can be made out of one pepper. Make sure the ridges are in the middle of the flowers.

2 A baby corn or a carved carrot is inserted on top of a skewer.

3 Use little cutters to make flowers from peppers, carrots, etc.

4 Fill celery stalks with cream cheese or other fillings.

法國玫瑰

玫瑰的花瓣是圓的。切雕時花瓣應該上薄逐漸往下增厚。

1. 用小尖刀的刀鋒雕圓花瓣，花瓣與花瓣應相連。
2. 雕第二層花瓣前，先挖除一圈餘肉，再將表面修圓而平滑。
3. 第二層的花瓣與第一層交錯。
4. 重覆作法 **2**、**3** 直到花心。可染上顏色以增效果。

French Rose

The secret of success in this rose is to make the petals round. In nature, petals are thin at the top, gently rounded, and thicker at the base for stability.

1. Using only the tip of the knife, make round petals without leaving space in between.
2. Cut around the radish and trim the rough edges, leaving indentations for the next row of petals. Remove excess radish.
3. The next row of petals are placed in between the petals of the first row.
4. Repeat steps **2** and **3**. Continue to repeat these steps until you reach the flower center. Color for added interest.

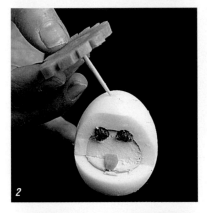

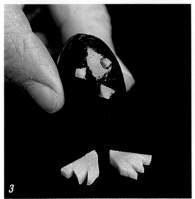

蛋人和企鵝

蛋人和企鵝是宴會中頗具趣味性的盤飾，任何年齡的孩子都喜歡。

1 熟蛋的較寬端切平做底部。直、橫各切一刀，取出一塊成臉部。

2 黑胡椒粒、葡萄乾或丁香嵌入做眼睛。紅椒或紅蘿蔔做舌頭。紅蘿蔔片或其他材料做帽子即成蛋人。

3 黑橄欖做企鵝頭。眼睛、嘴和腳可用紅蘿蔔來做。

4 熟蛋底部切平。用牙籤插入頭和腳，再插切半的黑橄欖做為二隻手即成企鵝。

Egg Man and Penguin

Egg men and penguins are great party teasers for kids of all ages.

1 Slice out a flat bottom on the widest end of a hard boiled egg. Remove a 90° angle wedge from one side to make a face.

2 Insert black peppercorns, raisins, or cloves for eyes. A pepper or carrot for a tongue. A carrot slice or your own creation for the egg man's hat.

3 Penguin's head is a black olive. Use carrot for eyes, beak, and feet.

4 Slice out a flat bottom from a hard boiled egg. Attach the head, feet, and black olive halves for wings with toothpicks.

花瓶

有時簡單就是美。

1 選用結實且形狀美好的茄子，用花模在茄子上壓花，以使嵌入橘子皮或不同果蔬的壓花。

2 取出壓花模後，插入小尖刀由皮下將花挖出。

3 刻細長條紋做為花莖與葉子。

4 去皮僅留少許綠色的藤壺瓜，亦可做成一個美麗的花瓶。

Vase

At times, simplicity is more stunning than abundance.

1 A well shaped, very firm eggplant is necessary. Use cutters to make flowers in eggplant and citrus peels. Replace the eggplant cutouts with citrus flowers or other fruit / vegetable flowers.

2 To remove the cutouts from the eggplant, insert a sharp knife, cutting just under the skin.

3 Cut narrow strips on the eggplant to create stems and leaves.

4 A peeled acorn squash can make a lovely vase, especially when a little green is left in the ribs.

魚和旋轉片

檸檬魚媽媽和小青檸檬魚使盤飾看起來格外生動。

1. 檸檬一端切除一三角塊成魚嘴，下面切除一塊（約0.5或1公分厚）成魚的底部。切塊上再切除三角片成魚尾。檸檬莖端切一長方形溝以便插入魚尾。
2. 用剝皮刀或尖形雕刀刻出魚眼即成檸檬魚。
3. 用剝皮器在檸檬皮表面刻細長條紋後，切片。每片切刀口至中心。
4. 可扭轉檸檬片後放在盤內或插在杯口上。

Fish and Twists

A lemon mama and little lime babies make an awesome display.

1. On one end of lemon, cut a large "V" for a mouth. Cut a 1/4" or 1/2" (0.5cm or 1cm) slice off the side of a lemon to create the base. Cut a rounded "V" in the end of the above slice for a tail. Cut a rectangle in the stem end of the lemon to insert tail.
2. A stripper or v-shaped-blade carving tool makes fish lips and eyes.
3. To make the twist, remove lengthwise strips of peels with a stripper. Slice the lemon then cut each slice to the center.
4. Twist the slices to border plates or hang on the side of a glass.

梨子盤飾 · PEAR GARNISH

梨鴿

此盤飾雖簡單，但效果卻不輸於複雜且費時的盤飾。

1 選用形狀好且彎曲適宜的梨子。將梨直立，二邊切楔形片（切二斜刀，成 "V" 形，相交於中央）做翅膀。

2 切數層楔形片，向後推並用牙籤固定。

3 丁香嵌入做鴿眼，即成梨鴿。

4 亦可將黃色彎頸的瓜類直切二半。如上法做出翅膀。用丁香做眼睛。胡蘿蔔做腳。

Pear Quail

This very simple little bird draws as much attention as any time consuming piece.

1 Choose a well shaped pear with a nice curved stem. Cut wedges in the sides to make wings (see p. 41).

2 Cut wedges out of the first wedges, slide all the pieces back, secure them with picks.

3 Insert cloves for the eyes, OR

4 Cut a yellow crocked-neck squash in half. Do wings the same way as quail in steps 1 and 2. Insert cloves for eyes, carved carrot for feet.

哈密瓜花瓶

花瓶作法參考第41頁〝蘋果鳥〞，玫瑰花作法參考第35頁〝法國玫瑰〞，黃色花作法參考第6頁〝沙拉器〞，蒜菊花做法參考第32頁。

Cantaloupe Vase

Instructions for the details may be found on the following pages:

Vase, page 41 (Apple Bird), French Rose, page 35, Squash Flower, page 6 (Saladacco), Leek Mums, page 32

蘋果盤飾 · APPLE GARNISH

蘋果鳥

蘋果鳥和水果、蛋、蛋糕或插花一起擺飾，可增添效果。

1　蘋果的最平面，切下一塊楔形片，留做鳥頭，此切面當底部。

2　頂部連續切出數層楔形片。每切一片同時往後推即成鳥尾。

3　另左、右二面也同法切楔形片以切出鳥的翅膀。

4　留下來的鳥頭以丁香為眼，以紅蘿蔔做為鳥嘴，頭用牙籤固定。灑上檸檬汁或塗上吉利膠，不僅可固定位置，且可防止變色。

● 楔形片切法：切二斜刀，成 "V" 形，相交於中央，此切片即為楔形片。

● 吉利膠，一包吉利丁加入1/2杯的水，待4分鐘變軟後，再加熱調勻即成。盤飾若有破裂可浸入吉利膠內取出，待涼即黏結在一起。

Apple Bird

Fruits, eggs, cakes, or floral arrangements are enhanced by this handsome bird.

1　Cut a 3/4" (2cm) wide wedge from the flattest side of an apple for the bird's base.　This wedge becomes the head.　Directly opposite of this wedge, make another wedge as wide as possible to create a handsome tail.

2　Cut wedges out of the tail wedge.　Then slide each one backward a little so as to assure that all cuts are complete.

3　Cut wings on each side, following the directions in step *2*.

4　Use cloves for eyes, and a carrot for beak.　Fasten the head with a toothpick.　Sprinkle the bird with lemon juice or cover it with gelatin glue in order to hold the bird together, and also to prevent discoloration.

● Gelatin glue:　In a small sauce pan, sprinkle 1 envelope of plain gelatin over 1/2 cup cold water.　Let stand 4 minutes to soften.　Stir over heat until the small granules dissolve.　Dip the pieces to be glued or glazed into the gelatin.　They set almost immediately when chilled.

柚皮玫瑰

美麗的盤飾並不一定需要花費錢。通常丟棄不用的柚皮內白肉可用來做此精緻而耐用的玫瑰花。

1 薄薄去除葡萄柚的外皮，儘量不要削到白色的內皮。

2 沿著根部，連續不斷將白色內皮片成一長薄片。

3 直至另一端的3/4處止。

4 由根部緊緊捲起六圈成花心。繼續繞成花狀。染色後看起來像天鵝絨。

Peel Rose

Serving food beautifully need not cost money. The white portion between the skin and flesh of a grapefruit, usually thrown away, can be used for this sturdy yet delicate rose.

1 Remove a very thin layer of the grapefruit skin, leaving as much white portion as possible.

2 Cut a circle from the top, leaving the stem end in the grapefruit.

3 Try not to break while continuously cutting until 3/4 way to the other end. Break off the peel.

4 Start with the stem end, rolling up the first six twists tightly to create the center of the rose. Relax the rest of the turns. Place the end of the circle on a flat surface and set the rolled portion in the center to create a flower in bloom. This rose looks like velvet when colored.

哈密瓜盤飾 · CANTALOUPE GARNISH

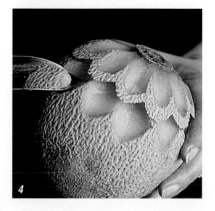

花

圓形裝飾雕刀（參考第7頁）相當實用且效果佳。它可去蘋果核，挖空黃瓜或意大利瓜。

1 用圓形裝飾雕刀沿著莖在外皮刻一個圓圈。

2 挖一圈花瓣。

3 沿著花瓣再雕一圈。如果切口不相連接，用刀切，使連接。

4 外圍交錯刻第二層花瓣。如此重覆步驟，續雕花瓣至整個雕完。

Melon Flower

The U deco knife (see p. 7) is a superb and practical tool for garnishing; coring apples, and hollowing out cucumbers or zucchini.

1 By using the U deco knife around the vine end, a circle is cut through the peel only.

2 Scoop out the insides of the petals.

3 Outline the petals. If cuts are not connected, cut them so they are.

4 In between each petal of the first row, cut out the next row of petals. Continue this process until the fruit is completed.

鯨魚

鯨魚比普通的籃子富有趣味性。

1 西瓜一端切半圓做頭,另一端刻尾巴。

2 切除頭和尾巴之間多餘的西瓜,並在頭部刻出魚眼。

3 挖一個洞,插入蔥刷做為鯨的噴水口。

4 處理過的葡萄串置鯨魚內有意想不到的效果。

  葡萄的處理:將葡萄浸入略打過的蛋白裡使外皮產生黏性,再撒上白糖、有色糖或果凍粉即成。

Whale

The whale is much more whimsical than an ordinary basket.

1 Cut a half circle near an end of a melon for the head. Then cut on the other end for the tail.

2 Cut the two sides of the melon to connect the tail and the head. Pull the melon apart. Draw eyes with a stripper or v-shaped-blade carving tool.

3 Use the round end of the large carving tool to cut a hole for inserting a green onion brush as the spout.

4 Frosted grapes, skewered in the whale, make a lovely presentation. These are made by coating the grapes with lightly beaten egg whites. Let them set for a few minutes until the grapes are just sticky. Then sprinkle plain or colored sugar, or jello powder over the grapes' surface.

西瓜盤飾 · WATERMELON GARNISH

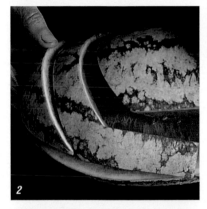

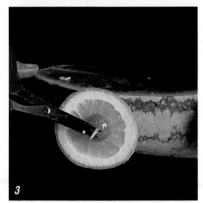

嬰兒車

這種嬰兒車不僅適於嬰兒慶生會上採用，同時亦可做為最佳賀禮。

1. 用圓形裝飾雕刀（參考第7頁）刻出車蓬，並以挖球器在瓜上挖洞後，填入葡萄或櫻桃以添趣味。
2. 瓜切半至車蓬處止，剝下後切出把手。
3. 用牙籤固定橘子片及櫻桃做車輪。
4. 用牙籤將把手固定在西瓜上。車上可填入沙拉器做出的花（參考第6頁）。

Baby Duggy

The buggy is ideal at a shower or baby party; also a good gift, too.

1. The U deco knife (see p. 7) is used to cut the hood of the buggy. To add more interest, use a melon baller to make holes in the hood and place grapes or cherries in the scallops.
2. Cut the melon horizontally in half up to the hood. Pull the melon apart. Cut handles from outout of the melon
3. Secure orange slices, cherries with toothpicks as wheels and hub caps.
4. Skewer the handle on securely. May fill with turnip flowers made on the Saladacco (see p. 6).

湯美凱利 Tomi Carey **45**

湯姆火雞

此盤飾可由萬聖節應用全聖誕節，成為餐桌上的焦點。

1 瓜的正面刻出脖子，背面最高處做尾巴。連接脖子和尾巴。切除多餘西瓜。

2 檸檬上切長方形溝以便插在脖子上做火雞頭。葡萄或橄欖切半做眼睛。紅蘿蔔做嘴巴。

3 用牙籤固定頭。葡萄串做喙下的肉垂。

4 椒片、洋菇、金橘、蔥刷、西瓜球、醃黃瓜、橄欖、青花菜、白花菜、熱狗片、起司等皆可插入竹籤做為雞尾的裝飾。

Tom the Turkey

During the pumpkin season, this turkey can be used as the centerpiece from Halloween through Yuletide.

1 For a guideline, first cut out the shape of the neck in the center of the "front" of a melon, as shown. For the tail, mark the highest portion directly on the "back" of the melon. Cut the other two sides from the neck to the tail. Pull the melon apart. Hollow out the watermelon.

2 Hollow out a rectangle on the side of a lemon or a lime in which to insert the turkey's neck. Use grapes or olives for eyes, and a carrot for the beak, hold them in place with toothpicks.

3 Secure the head on the neck; use a small bunch of grapes for the wattle.

4 Use skewers or similar sticks for the tail. Insert vegetables on skewers to create plumage. Examples: pepper slices, mushrooms, kumquats, green onions, melon balls, pickles, olives, broccoli, cauliflower, hot dog slices, cheese, etc.

哈密瓜盤飾 · CANTALOUPE GARNISH

天鵝

天鵝可選用任何尺寸的瓜類。可用來展示水果或單獨陳列成為餐桌的中心裝飾。

1 瓜上刻S形成鵝頭。

2 由頭向二邊切三個逐漸上升的尖形為翅膀。最後二刀在背部的相交點，儘可能放低。

3 用剝皮器或尖形雕刀刻眼睛。將瓜剝開，挖除內部。去除翅膀和頭內的果肉，填入水果或雕好的花。

4 鴨子做法：哈密瓜底部平切下一片，刻成鴨頭形狀後插在瓜上。其餘做法同蘋果鳥（參考第41頁）。

Swan

This swan, which can be made from any sized melon, is a handsome garnish. It can be part of a fruit display or a centerpiece by itself.

1 Cut an "S" to outline the top of a swan's head and the start of wings.

2 Then, continue to cut 3 wing feathers on each side of the melon, each wing progressively higher. Cut very low in the back of the melon where the third pair of wing feathers meet.

3 Use a stripper or v-shaped-blade carving tool to carve an eye. Pull the melon apart and clean out the seeds. Cut flesh from wings and head. Fill the swan with fruits or carved flowers.

4 The duck decoy is made in the same way as the Apple Bird (see page 41) except that the head is a flat piece sliced off from the bottom. Carve the shape of a duck's head as desired and attach it with several toothpicks.

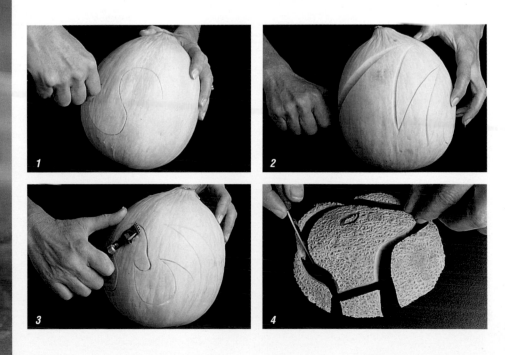

西瓜盤飾 · WATERMELON GARNISH

孔雀開屏

孔雀做法類似火雞（參考第46頁），只需稍加修改就可做出不同的鳥。讀者可自行變化。

1 瓜正面切出頭小、脖子略彎的孔雀形。

2 續切至西瓜背面的最高點。沿切紋剝開西瓜，去除頭後瓜肉。

3 眼部挖洞嵌入紅蘿蔔做眼睛。頭上插上滿天星或切細絲的蔥段。

4 竹籤上串插多種顏色的糖果、水果或蔬菜做為尾巴。

Peacock

The Peacock is made in the same manner as the turkey (see p. 46) providing ideas on how you can create any style bird by changing only a few features.

1 At the "front" of a melon, cut a head that is small and a neck that is long and slightly curved.

2 Cut to the very top at the "back" of the melon. Pull melon apart. Clean flesh away from the head.

3 Clean out the melon. For the eye, take out a core with the small carving tool and replace it with a carrot core. Insert baby's breath or green onion brush on the top of the head.

4 For the tail; skewer colorful candies, fruits, or vegetables for single, double, or triple layers.

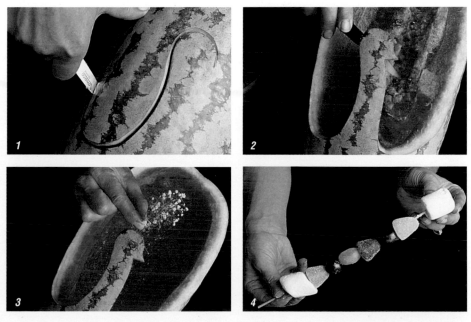

西瓜盤飾 · WATERMELON GARNISH

水果籃

檸檬、番茄或任何大小的瓜類做成的花籃，可填滿花朵或食物，相當受歡迎。

1 在西瓜上用有色膠帶貼出花籃和把手的位置。用尖形裝飾雕刀（參考第7頁）沿著膠帶雕一圈相連且深至核心的鋸齒紋。並切出把手，雕出花籃形狀。

2 剝除多餘外皮及瓜肉。

3 挖空花籃內的瓜肉。

4 剝除把手上瓜肉，保留一些紅色，以增加色彩。

Basket

A basket is a hit whether it is made from a lemon, lime, tomato, or any sized melon, filled with flowers or food.

1 Use tape as guidelines for the edges and the handle of the basket. Follow the tape with a V deco knife (see p. 7) by inserting it into the center of melon. Be sure to connect all V cuts.

2 For a different look, cut away only the peel along the tape, so red flesh is exposed instead of hollowing out the melon as done in the Melon Swan (see p. 48).

3 Remove all flesh if an empty basket is desired.

4 Remove the flesh from the handle, leaving a little pink showing for both stability and color.

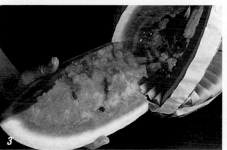

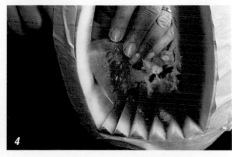

鳳梨盤飾 · PINEAPPLE GARNISH

天鵝

製作天鵝時，保持尾巴高舉，鵝首側向一邊，以表現天鵝的個性。

1　鳳梨底部切除一片以便置於莒上，使綠葉部份高舉做尾巴。

2　兩側切片至底部2.5公分處止做翅膀。塞入小塊的底部切片使翅膀張開。

3　近底部切掉一塊，使插入彎曲的瓜做為頭。嵌入丁香粒做眼睛。

4　香蕉亦可做天鵝頭。香蕉上刻羽毛紋和眼睛，再用竹籤將頭固定。

Swan

Keep swan's tail high and the head positioned to the side for more character.

1　Cut the bottom off a pineapple so the top greenery sticks up in the air to make a handsome tail.

2　Cut a straight line 1" (2.5cm) from the bottom on each side of the pineapple to make wings. Insert a piece of pineapple, cut from the bottom in step **1**, to hold the wings out.

3　Cut away a portion of the pineapple to insert a yellow crocked neck squash for the head. Insert cloves for the eyes.

4　A banana also makes a handsome swan's head. Use large carving tool to make gashes in banana to look like feathers. Cut eyes. Hold head on with skewers.

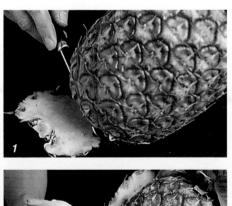

什錦水果盤飾 · FRUIT GARNISH

卡門

卡門是最佳的餐桌中心盤飾。讀者可自行創造其它的人物和聖誕老人或舞者等。

1 豐滿西瓜的底部切掉一片，刻U形裙花邊。

2 用小尖刀刻裙褶。

3 選用適當形狀的瓜類做身體，用剝皮刀或尖形雕刀刻出領口，去除領口內果肉使喉嚨露出，與領口平行再刻一圈。

4 在蘋果面上用刀鋒刻出臉形，去除多餘果皮，灑上檸檬汁以防變色，以香蕉當手臂。

5 西瓜底部的切片做成帽子，插上鳳梨頭部或其它綠葉做帽飾，也可插上花朵。全身用牙籤牢牢固定。葡萄、小花等皆可用來裝飾。小花可用沙拉器製作，很方便。（參考第6頁）。

Carmen

Carmen is the leader of all centerpieces. She can provide ideas on how other characters, like "Santa Claus" to "A Man and Woman Dancing" can be created.

1 Cut off the bottom of a nice plump melon for Carmen's skirt. Use the U deco knife (see p. 7) to open up the skirt.

2 The sharp-pointed knife is perfect for making pleats by cutting horizontal lines about 1" (2.5cm) deep. Cut through rind at this point to remove the peel.

3 The bodice is from any melon that has the correct shape. Use a stripper or V-shaped-blade carving tool to cut the neck line and a parallel line under it. Cut away the flesh to expose the throat.

4 Use the tip of a knife to draw Carmen's face on an apple. Peel away all but the features. Squeeze lemon juice on her face to prevent discoloring. Use bananas as arms.

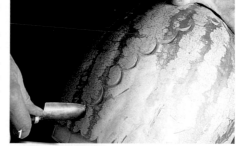

5 Use the bottom of the melon for her hat. Fasten a pineapple top or other greenery on top of the hat. Add flowers as desired. Attach the parts together securely. Decorate her with a grape stole, flowers around her waist, etc. The Saladacco (see p. 6) is handy to create flowers quickly.

湯美凱利 Tomi Carey **57**

世外桃源

這一道盤飾乍看之下是否熱鬧有趣？以各種蔬果雕飾成與世無爭的花果山，雖須費時較多，但若能自己動手作出一幅生動、活潑，看了不覺莞爾的畫面，未嘗不是一件樂事。

花果山做法參考第60、61頁。

A Secluded Paradise

This is a fantasy garnish. Although it takes time to carve this imaginary world by using fruits and vegetables, you will enjoy creating this ideal world.

See pp. 60, 61 for instructions to make this paradise.

世外桃源

1　蓮藕去皮以牙籤固定成岩石及山洞狀，取芋泥作湖邊，洋菜溶解後調綠色素當湖面，袖珍椰子樹插在蓮藕上。

2　白菜心染黃置岩石前，大黃瓜雕花果山字樣，以吉利膠（參考第78頁）固定於藕上，再黏於山前，綠色洋菜切小丁置山洞口，如瀑布狀。

3　將孫悟空（做法參考第62、63頁）及猴子（參考第64頁）分置山上及湖旁。

4　以紅、白高麗菜絲舖於四周，並將芋頭做成的竹籬放在湖前。

5　香蕉（參考第66頁）插上牙籤掛椰樹上，放上牛蒡做的小橋。

6　鵝（做法參考第68頁）插上牙籤置湖上，青蛙（參考第67頁）置湖旁。

7　長春藤掛上葡萄（參考第69頁）點綴於山洞前。

8　小菊及刺松分插於四周菜絲上，即成。

A Secluded Paradise

1 Pare lotus roots, secure them with toothpicks to make rocks and a cave. Use mashed taro to shape a lake. Color the dissolved green gelatin for the lake water. Insert a palm tree on a piece of taro.

2 Color the center portion of the nappa cabbage yellow; place in front of the rock. Carve characters for the name of the mountain on the cucumber and gelatin glue them on the slices of lotus root; secure the slices on the cave. Place chopped green gelatin in front of the cave to make a waterfall.

3 Place the Monkey King (pp. 62, 63) and monkeys (p. 64) on the mountain and beside the lake.

4 Place shredded white and red cabbage around the lake. Arrange the taro fence in front of the lake.

5 Secure some banana bunches (p. 66) with toothpicks on the palm tree. Use carrot or other vegetable as bridge.

6 Secure the geese (p. 68) with toothpicks on the lake. Place the frogs (p. 67) beside the lake.

7 Hang grapes on the ivy (p. 69), then decorate the ivy in front of the cave.

8 Arrange daisy and dill on the cabbage.

孫悟空

1 大型芋頭1個,由上端先切出頭形,並去除多餘部份。

2 切出肩膀、前胸及擺動的雙手。

3 切臀形及雙腳。

4 將頭戴金箍、胸配圍巾的孫悟空細部輪廓修飾出來。

5 取紅蘿蔔片黏貼做臉。

6 切出眼部凹陷、嘴型尖突的孫悟空臉形,將細牙籤塗黑插入當眼睛。

7 竹籤兩端塗黑成如意棒,旋轉貫穿孫悟空的手心。

8 蓮藕去皮削成岩石狀,以牙籤將做好的孫悟空固定其上即成。

The Monkey King

1 Sculpt a head on a large taro root by cutting away excess taro.
2 Cut the shape of the shoulders, chest, and hands.
3 Cut the shape of the buttocks and legs.
4 Cut the shape of the headband and scarf.
5 Cut and secure a rounded piece of carrot on the taro to make the face.
6 Cut deep-set eyes and protruding mouth. Color toothpicks black; cut them, then insert them for the eyes.
7 Color both ends of a skewer black; use it as a stick. Push skewer through the hand of the monkey by rotating it as it is inserted.
8 Pare a taro, then cut it into the shape of a rock. Attach the monkey to the rock with a toothpick.

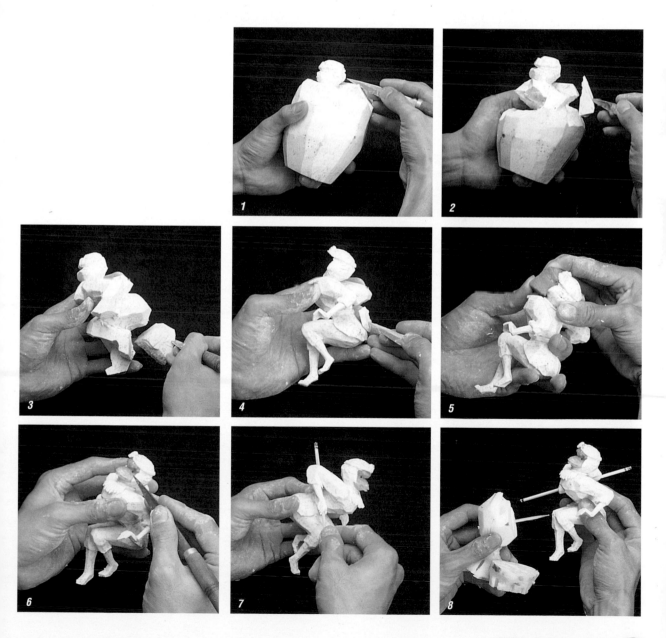

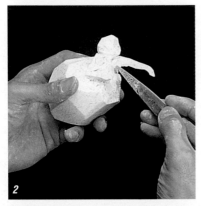

猴子

1 大型芋頭一個直切半,將切面朝前,在上端2/3處先切出頭形。

2 切伸長的左手及彎曲的右手。

3 再切出身體、臀部、腳部使呈趴蹲的姿勢。

4 底下剩餘芋頭當底座,另取一長條修圓滑做出翹起的尾巴,以三秒膠黏貼在尾部,紅蘿蔔做臉,細牙籤塗黑當眼睛,分別黏上即成。

● 猴子的生動在於頭、肩、背部要平,手腳均要靈活,才會生動,表現力的美,動物的自然神態變化多端,可預先拍照便於揣摩。

● 做好的盤飾,泡水時須特別注意,不同材質的花飾,儘可能分開來泡水,以免彼此受影響。

芋 頭 盤 飾 · TARO GARNISH

Monkey

1 Cut a large taro root lengthwise in half. Cut the shape of the head about one-third from the end of the taro on the opposite side of the flat side.

2 Cut left hand straight out. Cut and shape the bent right hand.

3 Cut to shape the body, buttocks and legs.

4 Use the excess on the bottom as a pedestal. Cut a long taro strip for a tail. A rounded piece of carrot is used as the face. Gelatin glue tail and face to the body of the monkey. Color toothpicks black to make eyes.

● To add interest, combine taro monkeys in different positions. If a large taro is used, cut it lengthwise in half instead of using a whole small taro.

● Pictures of monkeys may be taken beforehand to study and select the desired facial expression.

● Garnishes made from different materials should soak in water separately to prevent their affecting each other.

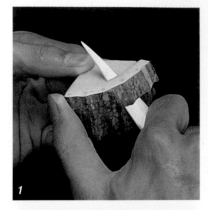

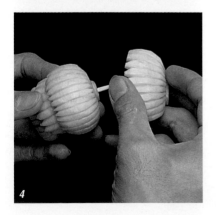

香蕉

1　南瓜一塊，分切4等份，削去皮。

2　將香蕉的輪廓大略修出來。

3　瓜面以尖刀劃出一根根並排的香蕉，再取尖雕刀將香蕉間的縫隙及底部多餘的瓜肉去除，並加以修整使香蕉形狀更立體。

4　可將做好的3、4串香蕉以3秒膠黏貼固定，再以牙籤串連在一起。

Bunches of Bananas

1　Cut a piece of yellow squash into quarters. Use a quarter of the squash and pare it.

2　Carve the squash into the shape of a bunch of bananas.

3　Use a sharp-pointed knife to draw lines for each individual banana. Use a V-shaped-blade carving tool to remove excess squash between bananas and on the bottom of the bananas. Trim to smooth surfaces.

4　Secure 3 or 4 banana bunches together with gelatin glue and toothpicks.

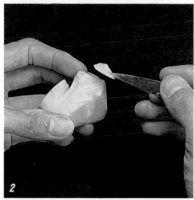

青蛙

1 南瓜一塊切成四等份後削去皮。

2 切除兩側呈尖形，做頭，隨後再切出 V 字形的蛙身並修出蛙腿，頭部並加以修整使兩側眼部輪廓現出。

3 將整雙青蛙修飾完整，嘴部向內切去一三角塊成張嘴狀。

4 做出手指與腳趾，眼部挖凹洞，牙籤塗黑，旋轉插入當眼睛即成。

Frog

1 Cut a thick slice of squash into quarters. Pare the squash.

2 Cut off both sides, to make a V-shape, this will be the head. Cut out a V-shaped body then trim to make the legs. Trim the head and score the shape of the eyes.

3 Trim the frog. Cut out a wedge to create an open mouth.

4 Cut to shape the fingers and toes. Cut indented holes on the outlined eyes; rotate the black toothpicks while inserting for the eyes.

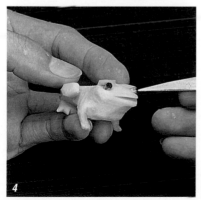

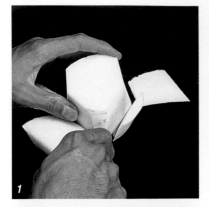

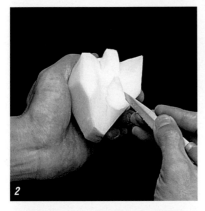

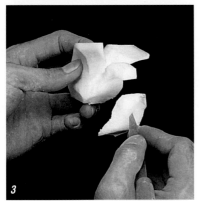

鵝

1 白蘿蔔切成五邊形。

2 切除二楔形片，使中央突起作頭，兩側高舉作翅膀。

3 切去鵝頭下及身體部份多餘的蘿蔔，將鵝頭及鵝身修飾完整。

4 在翅尾部份切出鋸齒紋，取紅蘿蔔修尖作嘴巴，細牙籤塗黑作眼睛，黏貼上即可。

Goose

1 Cut the daikon into a pentagon (5 sides).

2 Cut off two wedges to make the center stand out for the head, and two sides high for the wings.

3 Cut out excess daikon to smooth the head and the body.

4 Carve V-shaped grooves around the edge of the wings to give a feathered look. Use a piece of carrot shaped for the beak. Color toothpicks black and insert for the eyes.

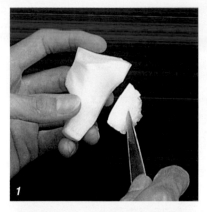

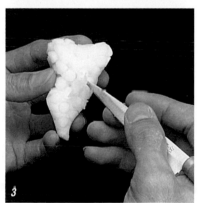

葡萄

1 白蘿蔔一段切出上寬下窄的倒三角形，並修出成串葡萄的輪廓。

2 以圓雕刀插入旋轉畫圓作葡萄，並使顆粒交錯。

3 再以尖刀挑出顆粒縫隙間多餘的蘿蔔使呈一顆顆立體的葡萄。

4 將葡萄修圓並染色。

Grapes

1 Cut a section of daikon into an inverted triangle. Carve the triangle into tho chape of a bunch of grapes.

2 Slowly rotate the daikon while inserting a curved-blade carving tool into the daikon to shape grapes. Alternate the position of the grapes until done.

3 Remove excess daikon between the grapes with a sharp-pointed knife.

4 Trim the grapes to round them, then color.

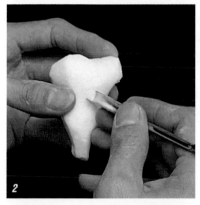

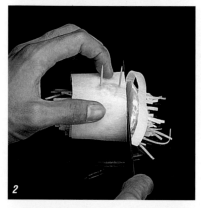

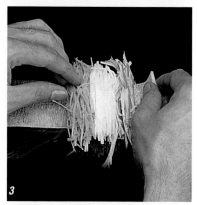

橘子花

1 一段白蘿蔔片出長薄片，一端鋪上少許紅、白蘿蔔絲及黃瓜絲，並將去皮的橘子置其上。

2 由橘子一端捲成筒狀，以數根牙籤固定，切除頭尾後再切片。

3,4 也可以紅、白蘿蔔及小黃瓜絲來做，亦十分美觀。

Tangerine Flowers

1 Cut a thin, long, and continuous slice around the length of a section of a daikon. Place a little loosely aligned shredded carrot, daikon, and cucumber across one side of the slice, then put a peeled tangerine on the strips.

2 Roll up the daikon slice from the tangerine side and secure with several toothpicks. Cut off excess portion on both sides then slice it.

3,4 It will also look beautiful by using shredded carrot, white radish and cucumber in the same way to make the garnish.

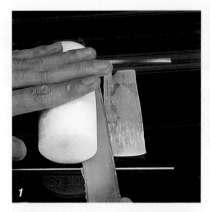

菊花

1 白蘿蔔取中段，兩旁置鐵針，片切25公分長的薄片。

2 將蘿蔔片對摺，由距開口1公分處向摺疊處連續斜刀切至全長2/3處後，逐漸將刀轉直，直刀切完。

3 由直切的一端捲起成花朵，底部插上牙籤固定，花朵中心處並塗上染料。

4 取南瓜屑或蛋黃屑置花朵中央當花蕊。

Chrysanthemum

1 Place skewers on both ends of a middle section of a daikon. Cut a 10" (25cm) long, thin slice around the length of the daikon, using the skewers as thin guides for thickness of slice.

2 Fold the slice lengthwise in half. Make diagonal cuts on folded edge to 1/2" (1cm) from opposite side. Starting at 1/3 from the opposite end, gradually change angle of cuts to end with straight vertical cuts.

3 Roll up the daikon from the vertical cut end to make a flower. Secure with toothpicks on the bottom. Color the center of the flower.

4 Sprinkle bits of pumpkin or chopped hard egg yolk in the center to make a pistil.

蠔味明蝦

材料：蝦、紅蘿蔔絲、蓮藕、巴西利、染色白菜心、刺松、孫悟空（參考第62、63頁）。

Shrimp in Oyster Sauce

Ingredients: Shrimp, shredded carrot, lotus root, parsley, colored nappa cabbage hearts, dill, and the Monkey King (see pp. 62, 63).

滷味花枝

材料：花枝、紅、白高麗菜絲、刺松、小菊花、鵝（參考第68頁）。

Stewed Cuttlefish

Ingredients: Cuttlefish, shredded red and white cabbage, dill, chrysanthemum, and goose (see p. 68).

臘味排骨

材料：排骨、番茄、蓮藕、巴西利、刺松、紅、白高麗菜絲、青蛙（參考第67頁）。

Salted and Smoked Pork Rib

Ingredients: Pork ribs, tomato, lotus root, parsley, dill, shredded red and white cabbage, and frog (see p. 67).

青黃蛋捲

材料：花蛋捲、高麗菜絲、刺松、蓮藕、袖珍椰子、香蕉（參考第66頁）、猴子（參考第64頁）。

Egg Rolls

Ingredients: Egg rolls, shredded cabbage, dill, lotus root, mini coconut, bunches of bananas (p. 66), and monkey (p. 64).

麻雀

1 小黃瓜削去薄皮，使綠色層保留，5公分處斜刀切斷備用。

2 由斜切面切出麻雀頭形，並於頭部後方挖除一三角塊，呈Ｖ字型，使頭與背明顯分出。

3 另一端再斜切一塊成尾形，將整隻麻雀修飾完整。

4 取牙籤塗黑當眼睛及嘴巴，分別裝上，再取一支直立，一支彎折的牙籤插入當腳即成。

Sparrow

1 Lightly pare a gherkin cucumber, leaving outside green. Diagonally cut a section, 2" (5cm) from the end.

2 Cut a head from the side of the diagonal cut. Cut out a small wedge behind the head to distinguish the head and the back.

3 Make a diagonal cut from the other end of the sparrow to make the tail. Trim the sparrow.

4 Color toothpicks black for the eyes and beak. Insert one straight, one bent toothpick for the legs.

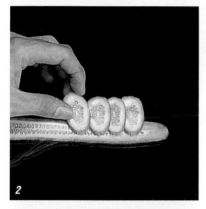

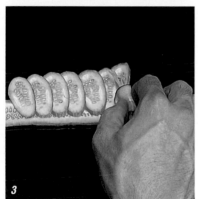

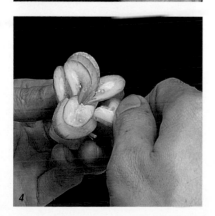

花

1 小黃瓜直切半，片切長薄片。
2 上鋪7片切好的斜薄片。
3 一端置少許的紅蘿蔔絲當作花心，並由花心處一端捲起成花朵，底部穿上牙籤固定。
4 將黃瓜片一片片翻開即可。

Flowers

1 Cut a cucumber lengthwise in half. Lengthwise, cut a thin, long slice.
2 Arrange 7 slightly overlapping slices of cucumber along the top of the long slice.
3 Place a little shredded carrot on one end of the slice to make the flower center. Roll up the slice, starting at the end with the carrot. Secure the bottom of the flower with toothpicks.
4 Open up the cucumber slices.

一帆風順

做好的帆船配上各式花草、魚、蝦、鱘魚、烏龜及海浪，組合成一幅熱鬧有趣的海洋奇觀，這種盤飾在海鮮類筵席中出現，頗為別緻。

帆船做法參考第78頁。

蝦做法參考第82頁。

魚卵魚做法參考第80頁。

香魚做法參考第79頁。

烏龜做法參考第81頁。

The Sailboat in Ocean

Decorate the sailboat with flowers, parsley grass, fish, shrimp, turtle. Waves make an interesting and spectacular ocean scene.

Instruction details are on the following pages:

Sailboat, page 78.

Shrimp, page 82.

Fish with eggs, page 80.

Fish, page 79.

Turtle, page 81.

帆船

1　赤鯮魚由背部剖開使腹部相連，取出大骨。

2　魚腹朝下，兩旁以小杯撐住（蒸好的魚才能直立，不致倒塌），連同魚骨入鍋蒸5分鐘，至肉剛熟。

3　鮭魚皮攤開置板上，釘上釘子蒸1分鐘。

4　將細竹與魚骨綁成十字型。

5　蒸好的魚皮，兩面以吉利膠＊黏於魚骨上成帆狀。

6　做好的帆插於胡蘿蔔上固定，置於魚身中央，並注入吉利膠，待冷使其凝結，再淋吉利膠於帆及魚身以增加光澤，以紅櫻桃當眼睛，取奶油在魚帆及眼部四周擠花，帆上以熟蝦及櫻桃點綴。

＊　吉利膠：吉利丁6大匙及溫水3杯置容器，調勻後可將容器置熱水中使膠呈液狀或置冰水中使膠呈固體狀。調整水溫以取得所需黏度的膠。

Sailboat

1　Lightly cut the back of a snapper, being careful not to cut through the belly. Remove the backbone.

2　Hold the fish, belly side down; place two small cups in the open back so that it will stand after steaming. Steam the fish and the bone for about 5 minutes or until cooked. Remove the bone.

3　Pin down the opened skin of a salmon on a small board; steam it for 1 minute. Remove the skin.

4　Tie a narrow stick on the fish bone to make a cross spar.

5　Attach the fish skin on both sides of the bone with gelatin glue* to form the sail.

6　Secure the sail on a piece of carrot; place on the snapper. Pour gelatin glue into the fish; let it cool until firm. Spread gelatin glue on the sail and the fish body to add luster. Add cherries for the eyes. Use soft butter around the sail and the eye. Decorate the top of the mast with a cooked shrimp and a cherry.

*　Gelatin Glue: Dissolve 6 tablespoons gelatin in 3 cups warm water in a container. The container of dissolved gelatin may be soaked in hot water to liquefy, or in cold water to solidify. Water temperature may be adjusted to mix gelatin to the desired consistency.

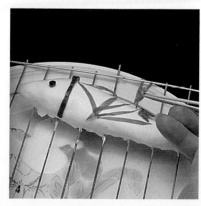

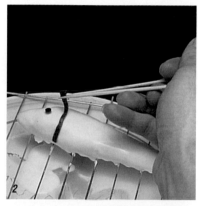

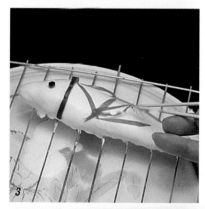

香魚

1 香魚去腸泥洗淨，蒸熟後置網上，淋上調好的吉利漿（吉利丁4大匙加溫水1杯先調勻，再加沙拉醬1杯拌勻，以紗布過濾，去除泡沫），放入冰箱冷卻。

2 取出後續淋一次吉利漿，再放入冰箱冷卻，如此反覆數次至魚身呈乳白色並有光澤，以黑橄欖、紅椒漬當眼睛及鰓。

3 將燙熟的蔥以刀尖劃成花葉，置魚身上。

4 擺上蝦尾當花裝飾。

Fish

1 Clean the fish and steam until cooked. Mix well one cup dissolved gelatin (Mix 4T. gelatin with 1 c. warm water) and one cup of mayonnaise; strain the mixture through a cheese cloth to remove bubbles. Spread the mixture on the fish and refrigerate until cool.

2 Spread the mixture on the fish again and refrigerate until cool. Repeat this procedure three times or until the fish is white and lustrous. Use a black olive for the eye and red pepper for the gill.

3 Use the tip of a knife to cut the cooked green onion into leaves. Arrange the leaves on the fish.

4 Use shrimp tails as flowers to complete the decoration.

魚盤飾 · FISH GARNISH

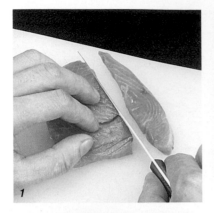

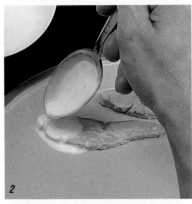

魚卵魚

1 鮭魚切0.5公分薄片。

2 將魚片蒸1分鐘取出待冷，取寬的一端作魚頭，淋上調勻的吉利漿（吉利丁4大匙加溫水1杯先調勻，再加沙拉醬1杯拌勻以紗布過濾，去除泡沫）待冷續淋一次，如此反覆數次至呈乳白色狀。

3 以黑橄欖、紅椒漬當眼睛及鰓。

4 再淋上吉利膠（吉利丁2大匙加溫水1杯調勻）使其更有光澤，以奶油在魚身四周擠花，上置黑魚子及紅魚子即成。

Fish with Eggs

1 Slice salmon into 1/4" (0.5cm) thick slices.

2 Steam the fish for 1 minute; allow to cool. Use the wide side of the sliced fish for the head. Mix well one cup dissolved gelatin (Mix 4T. gelatin with 1 c. warm water) and one cup of mayonnaise. Spread the gelatin and mayonnaise mixture on the fish; let it cool. Repeat the spread process several times or until the fish is white.

3 Use a black olive for the eye; red pepper for the gill.

4 Sprinkle gelatin glue (Mix 2T. gelatin with 1c. warm water) to add luster. Decorate the edge of the fish with soft butter. Put black and red caviar on the fish.

龜

1 香菇煮熟，取出鑲上魚漿抹平。

2 取紅蘿蔔刻出龜頭、腳及尾巴，並以黑芝麻當眼睛，分別裝上，入鍋蒸5分鐘，待冷淋上吉利膠（吉利丁2大匙加溫水1杯調勻）使其固定。

3 以奶油在龜殼上擠花紋。

4 將紅魚子置其上即成。

Turtle

1 Evenly spread fish paste on a presoaked and cooked Chinese black mushroom.

2 Carve carrot for the head, legs, and tail. Secure them on the mushroom with toothpicks. Use black sesame seeds for the eyes. Steam the turtle for 5 minutes; let it cool. Sprinkle the gelatin glue (Mix 2T. gelatin with 1c. warm water) on the turtle to set.

3 Decorate the turtle shell with butter.

4 Put red caviar on the turtle.

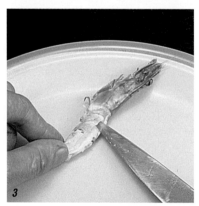

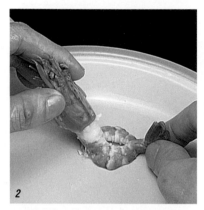

蝦

1 蝦煮熟以冷水沖涼，取下蝦頭備用，蝦身去殼留尾，由背部至腹部剖開，但兩端各留1分分不切。

2 由蝦腹翻開，裝上蝦頭，使頭尾翹起，小黃瓜橫切1.5公分長段，挖除中間瓜肉成凹狀，填入魚卵，置蝦腹中央，淋上吉利膠＊使其固定。

3 另一隻蝦插上細竹（以免煮時緊縮）煮熟，由蝦背劃一刀略打開。

4 淋上吉利膠後，將黑魚子置其上即成。

★ 吉利膠：吉利丁2大匙加溫水1杯調勻。

Shrimp

1 Rinse the cooked shrimp with cold water. Remove the head and shell, leaving the tail intact. Cut from the back through the belly, leaving 1/2" (1cm) from both ends connected.

2 Open the belly side of the shrimp. Put the head back on shrimp and let both the head and tail stand up. Cut gherkin cucumber into 5/8" (1.5cm) long pieces; remove the inside flesh and seeds; fill the cucumber with caviar. Put the cucumber on the center of the shrimp belly. Spread gelatin glue* to set.

3 Another arrangement: Insert a skewer into shrimp to keep it from shrinking during cooking. Cook shrimp. Make a cut on the back.

4 Sprinkle the shrimp with gelatin glue and put black caviar on it.

★ Gelatin glue: add 2 tablespoons of gelatin to 1 cup of warm water; mix well.

蛋盤飾 · EGG GARNISH

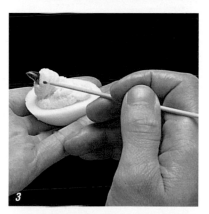

鳥

1 蛋煮熟去殼，由中央對切取出蛋黃，置篩子上，以飯杓壓平成粉末狀。

2 將蛋黃加少許沙拉醬，裝入擠花袋中成蛋黃醬，擠成鳥狀於蛋白上。

3 以黑芝麻、紅櫻桃分別作眼睛及嘴巴。

4 裝上大黃瓜片切成的翅膀及尾部，再將紅魚子置鳥身上即可。

Bird

1 Shell a hard boiled egg. Cut the egg lengthwise in half. Remove and mash the egg yolk.

2 Mix a little mayonnaise with the egg yolk. Form a bird by squeezing the mixture into the cavity of the egg white.

3 Use black sesame seeds for the eyes, cherry for the beak.

4 Carve the cucumber slice into wings and tail; secure them on the bird. Put red caviar on the bird.

蟹肉凍

材料：蟹肉、洋蔥末、白葡萄酒、鮮奶油、麵糊、菠菜汁、紅椒汁、香魚（參考第79頁）、巴西利、小花、魚卵。

Crab Meat Pat'e

Ingredients: crab meat, chopped onion, white wine, cream, flour paste, spinach juice, red pepper juice, the fish (p. 79), parsley, small flowers, and caviar.

蛋沙拉

材料：孔雀貝、蛋黃醬、魚卵、櫻桃、蛋鳥（參考第83頁）、小黃瓜、巴西利、孔雀貝殼。

Egg Salad

Ingredients: Mussel shell, egg yolk and mayonnaise paste, caviar, cherry, bird (p. 83), gherkin cucumber, parsley, and mussel shell.

龜與魚

材料：烏龜（參考第81頁）、魚卵魚（參考第80頁）、紅蔥頭、小花、巴西利、孔雀貝殼。

Turtle and Fish

Ingredients: Turtle (p. 81), fish with eggs (p. 80), scallions, small flowers, parsley and mussel shells.

蝦與水果沙拉

材料：蝦（參考第82頁）、蘋果、香瓜、木瓜、西瓜、千島汁、巴西利、紅蘿蔔花。

Shrimp and Fruit Salad

Ingredients: Shrimp (p. 82), apple, honey dew, papaya, watermelon, thousand island dressing, parsley, and carrot flowers.

水牛戲水

取石頭（或帶皮南瓜）、扁柏、榕樹、福建茶作背景，洋菜調綠色素當池塘，將水牛、白鶴、黃瓜片切出的荷葉及紅、綠櫻桃作成的荷花分別放置在池塘中，芋頭切雕出的牧童置牛背上，譜成一幅悠閒的田園記趣。

Buffalo Playing in Water

Rock (or pumpkin with skin) and branches from different kinds of plants may be used as background. Use color dissolved green gelatin as a pond. Put buffalo, white crane, water lily leaves (made from cucumber slices), and water lilies (made from red and green cherries) in the pond. A taro cowboy sits on the buffalo. These show a leisure, rural life.

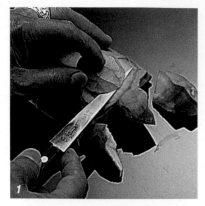

水牛

1 青蘿蔔1條直切半，先以尖刀切出牛頭輪廓，並劃出牛角，頭部後方再切除一塊，使牛角整個現出，牛身切呈八形，並削去所有的蘿蔔皮。

2 在左右牛角下方切出牛耳，同時將整個頭部輪廓修飾完整。

3 牛角上以尖刀劃出紋路。將牛身修飾圓滑，以紅辣椒套上火柴頭當眼睛，牛鼻以鐵線扣住即成。

Water Buffalo

1 Cut a green daikon lengthwise in half. Use sharp-pointed knife to cut and carve the head and score the horns. Remove excess flesh behind the head to reveal the horns. Cut the body into 八 shape. Pare the remainder of the green daikon.

2 Cut and carve the ears under the horns. Trim the head.

3 Score grooves on the horns, as shown. Trim the body. Cover the ends of matchsticks with red pepper for the eyes. Put a ring in the buffalo's nose.

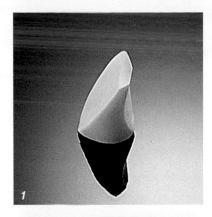

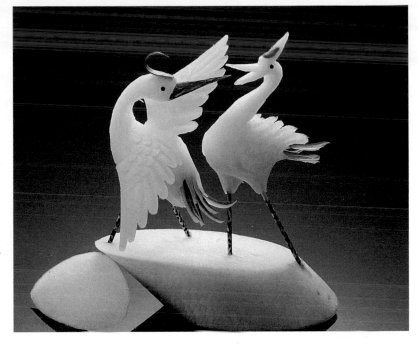

白鶴

1 白蘿蔔切除左右二片成錐形。

2 將切面朝前，以尖刀先切出鶴的嘴形和頭部輪廓，並以圓雕刀在頸部下畫圓（使線條弧度優美），續切出頸部。

3 切出鶴身、翅膀及鋸齒紋的尾部。以圓雕刀在兩側翅膀劃出羽毛紋，尾端則以尖雕刀雕出直條紋 ◐，取大黃瓜皮切出兩片鶴尾呈 ⋀ 形，重疊插入尾部（尾部須先切一橫溝，較好插），紅辣椒切斜薄片，黏於頭上當冠，黑芝麻當眼睛，牙籤塗黑插上當鶴腳即成。

● 白鶴的造型，可依個人喜愛任意變化，亦可另行作出一對高舉的翅膀，再以牙籤固定於鶴身，伸早振翅高飛狀。

White Crane

1 Diagonally cut off two pieces of the daikon, one piece from the right side and the other piece from the left side.

2 With a cut side facing you, use a sharp-pointed knife to cut the shape of the beak and head of the crane. Insert a curved-blade carving tool under the neck of the crane; cut the shape of the neck.

3 Trim the head, then cut the shape of the body, wings, and grooved tail. Carve feathers on the front part of the wing with a curved-blade carving tool; carve straight lines on the end part of the wings with a sharp-pointed knife, as shown ◐. Cut out two slices, as shown ⋀, from a cucumber skin. Cut a slit on the end part of the body; overlap and insert the cucumber slices into the slit for the tail of the crane. Diagonally cut a red chili pepper into slices; glue them on the head for a comb. Use black sesame seeds for the eyes, and black toothpicks for the crane's legs.

● Different shapes of crane may be carved according to individual preference. To make a crane in flight, carve the shape of two raised wings then affix them with toothpicks to the body.

玫瑰豆腐

將豆腐加蛋白調味後以刀壓成泥，蒸熟取出倒扣在盤上，上置黃蘿蔔花、茄子花及紅蘿蔔花（參考第91頁），取燙熟的芥菜當枝幹，芥菜梗作葉片（參考第155頁），以髮菜、洋菇、櫻桃圍邊，巴西利、紅蘿蔔片裝飾。

Bean Curd with Rose

Mix bean curd with egg white and seasoning. Mash and strain the bean curd; steam it in a bowl, then invert it on to a plate. Put a takuruan radish flower, a carrot flower (see p. 91) and an eggplant flower on the bean curd. Use cooked celery for branches, mustard green stalk for leaves (see p. 155). Arrange black moss, mushrooms, and cherries around the plate. Decorate with parsley and carved carrot slices.

紅蘿蔔盤飾 · CARROT GARNISH

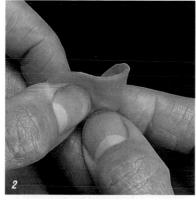

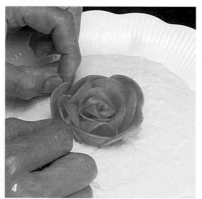

花

1,2 紅蘿蔔切半圓形薄片以鹽水泡軟，取一片內摺成花心。

3 在花瓣的1/3處向外捲一下，使花朵看起來高低層次分明，較立體，其他各片陸續圍繞花心做成花瓣後，將花插入豆腐。

4 外圍花瓣不須捲，直接插入豆腐即可，花朵大小可隨意。

Flowers

1,2 Cut a carrot lengthwise in half. Slice the carrot then soak the slices in salty water until soft. Curl one slice to make the flower's center.

3 At 1/3 from the edge of the petals; bend them outward to show the layers. Continue to arrange the other slices (petals) around the center. Place the flower in center of bean curd mound.

4 Insert the last layer into the bean curd; do not bend the petals outward. The flower may be sized as desired.

金盅三丁

素火腿、洋菇、紅蘿蔔分別切丁，調味炒熟，盛入金盅內（金盅做法參考第93頁），取紅蘿蔔絲及生菜墊底，上置金盅，以小黃瓜片及茄子（燙熟）分別作出枝幹及葉片，以髮菜當根部。

Diced Vegetable in Golden Cups

Stir-fry diced vegetarian ham, mushrooms and carrot until cooked, then season to taste. Put the mixture in the golden cups (see p. 93). Put shredded carrot and lettuce on a plate; place the golden cups on the bed of lettuce. Use gherkin cucumbers for the leaves, eggplant for the branches, and black moss for the root as garnish.

麵 粉 盤 飾 · FLOUR GARNISH

金盅

將水、麵粉各1杯加蛋1個及少許鹽調勻成麵糊備用。

1 取金盅模型入熱油鍋中燙一下，取出擦乾。
2 在模型外圍均勻地沾上麵糊。
3 入油鍋炸約30秒呈金黃色時取出。
4 待涼後，以手或小刀剝離。

Golden Cup

Mix one cup each of water and flour, one egg, dash of salt into a paste; set aside.

1 Carefully dip the mold in hot boiling oil. Remove and dry the mold.
2 Dip the mold into the flour paste to coat the outside.
3 Deep-fry the mold with flour paste for 30 seconds or until golden brown; remove it.
4 Let the mold cool. Remove the golden cup from the mold by hand or with a small knife.

水族世界

成群結隊、大大小小不同的魚，穿梭在岩石間，搭配砂石、海草及花飾，一幅奇妙的海底景觀，頓時顯現無遺。作品組合參考第96頁。

切雕要領：

1 持刀：學習切雕時，刀要以握筆的方式握穩。

2 選材：以選新鮮蔬果為要，不僅顏色鮮嫩且質地脆硬容易雕，但應注意避免斷裂，材料置放2〜3天後會變軟，不好切。

Sea World

Different fish swim among the rocks. Decorate with small rocks (chopped taro), parsley, and flowers, to create a wonderful sea world scene. For instructions to make the sea world, see p. 96.

Carving tips:

1 To hold a knife: Knife should be held stable like holding a pen.

2 To choose material: Only fresh vegetables and fruits should be used. Crispy vegetables or fruits with bright colors are easier to carve, but should be handled with care to prevent breakage. Materials can become soft in two or three days which will make carving difficult.

水族世界

1 蓮藕去皮，削成高低不規則的岩石，以牙籤固定。

2 將岩石置板上，以碎芋頭舖在岩石四周當砂石。

3 以巴西利圍繞當海草。

4,5,6 在岩石間分別將各種不同素材切雕成的魚（參考第99頁）以細竹插上固定，並擺上柚木皮做的船及黃瓜花裝飾（參考第106頁）。

Sea World

1 Peel a taro root. Cut the taro into irregular shapes of rocks; secure them with toothpicks.

2 Put the rocks on a board then put the chopped taro around them as small rocks.

3 Surround the small rocks with parsley as seaweed.

4,5,6 Arrange and secure different fish (see p. 99) among the rocks; decorate with boat and cucumber flowers (see p. 106) as desired.

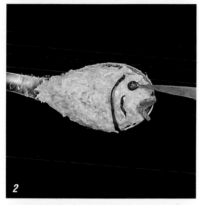

魚

1　湯匙預先塗油，蝦漿置其上抹平，裝上以紅蘿蔔切成的魚唇。

2　以香菇絲當鰓，紅辣椒套上巴西利莖作眼睛。

3　芋頭切1公分寬4公分長薄片，以刀尖切成背鰭及胸鰭，另切鱗狀薄片，將做好的背鰭、鱗片先裝上，並擺上蝦尾當魚尾。

4　最後裝上胸鰭，用油炸呈淡黃色即成。

Fish

1　Grease a tablespoon with oil. Put shrimp paste on the spoon and level off the paste. Use carrot for the mouth of the fish.

2　Use shredded, presoaked Chinese mushroom as gills. Insert a piece of parsley stalk into a piece of hot red pepper for the eyes.

3　Cut a taro root into thin strips of 1/2" (1cm) by 1 1/2" (4cm). Use the point of the knife to cut the strips into dorsal and pectoral fins. Cut the taro into thin slices to make the scales. Place the dorsal fins and scales on the fish. Use the tail of a shrimp for the fish tail.

4　Insert the pectoral fins, then deep-fry the fish until golden brown.

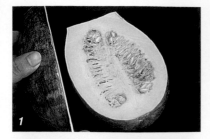

魚

1 南瓜切半。

2 去籽削皮後以尖刀劃出魚的輪廓，並去除多餘部份。

3 將魚鰭及魚尾部份修薄，使魚身突出。

4 取尖雕刀在魚鰭及魚尾兩面劃直條紋，在魚頭及魚身連接處傾斜45度挖凹洞，腹部約5公分處亦挖凹洞（分別用來裝魚鰓及鬚），再以圓雕刀在魚身雕鱗片。

5 將魚唇削薄使嘴形突出，並做出舌頭，取火柴頭以旋轉方式插入當眼睛，並以圓雕刀順眼睛球周圍劃一圈，去除多餘部份，使魚眼突出。

6 取剩餘南瓜切薄片及細長條，分別做出魚鰓及鬚，裝上即成。

● 除南瓜外，芋頭、青蘿蔔、紅蘿蔔、蕃薯、蘋果等都可用來切雕各種不同形狀的魚。

Fish

1 Cut a squash lengthwise in half.

2 Pare the squash and remove the seeds. Use a sharp-pointed knife to carve the shape of the fish on the squash. Remove excess squash.

3 Trim the fish fins and tail to make them thinner, and to show the body.

4 Use a V-shaped carving tool to carve indentations on both sides of the fins and tail. Hold the knife at a 45° angle; cut a groove on each side, between the head and body, for inserting the gills. Use the same procedure to cut grooves in the belly to insert the whiskers. With the curved-blade carving tool, carve scales on body of the fish.

5 Trim the fish to show the mouth and tongue. Rotate the matches while inserting them for the eyes.

6 Use excess pieces of squash to make the gills and whiskers.

● Taro root, carrot, potato, apple, etc., may be used to make different kinds of fish.

五味魷魚捲

材料：魷魚捲、紅蘿蔔、大黃瓜、茄子、魚板、大黃瓜魚盤飾（參考第107頁）。

Five Flavor Squid Rolls

Ingredients: squid rolls, carrot, cucumber, eggplant, steamed fish cake, and cucumber fish (see p. 107).

白灼風螺

材料：風螺、大黃瓜、魚板、高麗菜絲、巴西利、櫻桃、紅蘿蔔天鵝盤飾（參考第102頁）。

Boiled Conch

Ingredients: conch, cucumber, steamed fish cake, shredded cabbage, parsley, cherries, and carrot swans (see p. 102).

蛤蜊鑲魚漿

材料：蛤蜊、魚漿、大黃瓜、蟹肉魚板、高麗菜絲、巴西利、大黃瓜花盤飾（參考第109頁）、蘋果天鵝盤飾（參考第98,102頁）。

Clam Shell Filled with Fish Paste

Ingredients: clams, fish paste, cucumber, imitation crab cake, shredded cabbage, parsley, cucumber flowers (see p. 109), apple swan (see pp. 98, 102).

四拼

材料：洋火腿、豬肝、豆腐干、豬舌、番茄、巴西利、白蘿蔔魚盤飾（參考第98頁）。

Four Flavor Appetizers

Ingredients: ham, pig's liver, dried bean curd, pig's tongue, tomato, parsley, and daikon fish (see p. 98).

天鵝

1　紅蘿蔔12–16公分長，由上端切除左右2片。

2　面朝前處，續切除上下二塊蘿蔔，使中央一塊突起當鵝頭。

3　頭部左右兩旁各切出高舉的翅膀輪廓。

4　鵝身下端做出腳及底座，以圓雕刀在翅膀上雕羽毛。

5　翅膀尖端以尖雕刀刻直條紋，再由尾部上端兩邊平行切出0.5公分厚的翅膀。

6　修出翅尾並切除鵝頭後多餘的蘿蔔，取一小塊白蘿蔔修成嘴形，火柴頭當眼睛，分別裝上。

Swan

1　Cut a section of carrot, 5"-6" (12cm-16cm) long. Lengthwise, cut off two pieces from both sides of the carrot.

2　On the narrow side between the two cut sides, cut off two pieces, as shown, leaving the center intact to make the swan's head.

3　Carve the shape of the wings on both sides of the head. Trim the wings and remove the excess carrot.

4　Carve the legs and the pedestal. Carve the feathers with a curved-blade carving tool.

5　Carve straight lines on the wings with V-shaped carving tool. Cut wings, 1/4" (0.5cm) thick.

6　Cut the end of the tail to give a feathered effect. Remove excess carrot behind the swan's head. Trim a small piece of daikon into the shape of the beak; secure it on the swan. Use matches for the eyes.

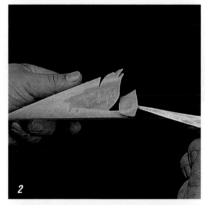

鳥

1 紅蘿蔔切10公分長三角塊。

2 依續切出鳥的嘴形、頭部、頸部、腹部及腳趾，並去除多餘的蘿蔔，使整隻鳥前身輪廓現出。

3 頭部後方切出翅膀及尾部，眼部以細竹穿洞，套入巴西利莖當眼睛。

4 做好的鳥，再分切薄片。

Bird

1 Cut a carrot into the shape of an isosceles triangle, 4" (10cm) long.

2 Starting from the right upper corner of short end of triangle, cut the shape of the beak, head, neck, belly, and claw of the bird. Remove excess carrot to reveal the bird.

3 Cut the shape of the wings and tail. Use a skewer to make holes then insert a stalk of parsley into the holes for the eyes.

4 Slice the carved bird to produce more birds.

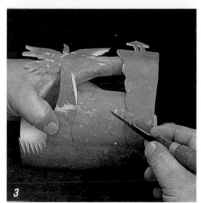

山水花鳥（一）

1　黃瓜10~12公分長，片出約0.5公分厚瓜皮，留3公分不片開。

2　末片開部份，切去部份外皮當底。

3　以尖刀刻劃椰樹、釣翁、山景等圖形輪廓。

4　剝除多餘的瓜皮，泡水後使用。

●　擺飾時，可在圖形背後插上牙籤撐著，使挺直。細嫩的大黃瓜用來切雕各種山水、鳥、魚、人物、花草等大幅圖案均能將細部輪廓一一刻劃出，綠白相間極為美麗。

Natural Scenery I

1　Cut a section of a cucumber, about 4" (10cm) long. Pare 1/4" (0.5cm) thick skin around the cucumber, leaving 1" (2.5cm) of skin attached to the flesh.

2　Cut off a piece of cucumber skin which is attached to the flesh, and serve the flat side of the remaining cucumber as the garnish base.

3　Draw pictures of a palm tree, a fisherman, a mountain scene, etc., on the skin of the cucumber.

4　Remove excess skin around design to reveal the design. Soak the cucumber in water before using it.

●　Toothpicks may be used behind the skin of the cucumber to prevent the pictures from bending. The tenderness of the cucumber ensures ease in carving the delicate designs of large pictures of mountains, birds, fish, people, flowers, etc.; the green and white color makes the pictures very beautiful.

山水花鳥（二）

1 黃瓜5-10公分長段，對切二半，取一半以尖刀在皮面劃出約1公分深的花型輪廓。

2 片約0.5公分厚瓜皮，底端留2公分切平當底。

3 剝除大片多餘的瓜皮。

4 以尖刀挑出花型中多餘的瓜皮，泡水後使用。

● 以大黃瓜皮切雕出椰樹、鳥、魚等各種小花式，可搭配其他的盤飾，配合用場一起擺飾。

Natural Scenery II

1 Cut a section of cucumber, 2" (5cm) to 4" (10cm) long, lengthwise in half. With a sharp-pointed knife, score 1/2" (1cm) deep flower design on the skin of the cucumber.

2 Pare off skin 1/4" (0.5cm) thick, leaving 1" (2.5cm) of skin intact with the flesh. Cut off a piece of cucumber, and serve the flat side of the remaining cucumber as the base of the garnish.

3 Remove the large piece of excess skin to reveal the flower.

4 Use a sharp-pointed knife to remove the excess skin from the petals.

● Palm trees, birds, fishes, etc., made from cucumber may be used as other garnishes.

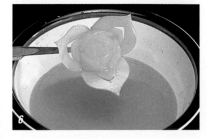

花（一）

1. 取蘿蔔或黃瓜頭，以尖刀在周圍等距切出5片花瓣，每片花瓣中央再劃二刀成⚄形，並以手略剝開。

2. 以尖刀沿圓周劃一圈。

3. 去除多餘的瓜肉使外層花瓣突出。

4. 在花瓣交錯間，同法做出第二層花瓣，如此反覆做數層，再將花心修圓。

5. 如使用白蘿蔔做，可染上喜愛的顏色。以牙籤沾染料在做好的花飾輕輕塗上，再用水沖一下，使色澤均勻。

6. 或色粉加水調勻，將花飾放入浸泡數分鐘即可。

Flower I

1. Cut a section from one end of cucumber or daikon. Use a sharp-pointed knife to cut five petals on the cucumber section. Make wedge cut on each petal to form ⚄ shape. Open up the petals, as shown.

2. Diagonally insert a knife between the petals and the center section; cut around the rim.

3. Remove the excess cucumber circle to make the petals stand out.

4. Cut second row of petals in between the petals of the first row. Repeat these procedures to make several rows of petals. Trim the flower center.

5. If daikon is used, it may be colored as desired. Use a toothpick to dip in food coloring then spread the color on a flower. Rinse the flower in water to spread the color evenly. OR

6. Mix food coloring and water well. Soak the flower in the mixed liquid for several minutes.

花（二）

1 紅蘿蔔取中段切☐形，以尖刀劃出5片高低不齊的花瓣。

2 沿圓周劃一圈。

3 取出多餘的蘿蔔，使花瓣突出，在花瓣交錯間，做出第二層花瓣，並去除多餘部份。

4 反覆做出層層花瓣即可。

● 此花可以白蘿蔔來做，再以牙籤沾染料在花瓣邊緣上色。。

Flower II

1 Cut a center section of carrot into a ☐ shape. Cut five uneven petals around the sides of the carrot.

2 Diagonally insert the knife between the petals and the center section; cut around the rim.

3 Remove the excess carrot circle to make the petals stand out. Cut the second row of petals in between the petals of the first row. Remove the excess carrot.

4 Repeat the procedure to make several rows of petals.

● If white radish is used for this garnish, use a toothpick, dipped in food coloring, to color the edges of the petals.

龍鳳

取大西瓜，在瓜皮描繪圖形，並刻劃出略有深度的線條輪廓，最後再片出瓜皮即可。

此種盤飾與一般冬瓜、南瓜等的雕飾法同，可配合各種用場，任意雕繪喜愛的圖形，西瓜宜選水份較少者（蒂頭乾）來做，才不易斷裂。

盤飾持久法：做好花飾宜置乾淨的清水或冰水中浸泡，欲隔夜使用須多次換水（同溫的水泡換）以保新鮮，亦可放入冰箱冷藏（切忌冷凍），並避免攪動，以防斷裂。

Dragon and phoenix

Draw desired picture on the skin of a large watermelon. Cut along the lines and carefully slide the cutting edge of knife underneath the design,then,remove the drawn picture.

Vegetable marrow, pumpkin, etc.,may be used in the same way to carve any desired shapes. Less juicier watermelons should be chosen to prevent the garnishes from breaking apart.

To make the garnish last longer: Garnish may be soaked in fresh water or ice water to keep fresh. If the garnish is to be soaked in water overnight, change water several times(only water of the same temperature should be used) or refrigerate the garnish (do not freeze it);and avoid stirring to prevent it from breaking.

食與藝

古今中外一道菜的色、香、質、味、形均離不
開藝。談到食，不僅要吃得好，吃得熱鬧，吃
得合時，更要吃得養身，吃得有雅趣。冷盤裝
飾即是烹飪的序曲，將內心對中國烹飪之理
想，融合了繪畫的技巧，切雕出各種精美花
飾，呈現在鏡盤上，充份表現出 "食" 與 "畫"
的整體藝術。

以各種不同的熟食物及果蔬為材料，擺飾出菊
花、蘭花、牡丹及梅花四款花式，透過鏡盤的
襯托，清新、脫俗的感覺，充分展現 "食上有
畫，畫上有食" 的食藝境界。

菊花：香菇、柳橙皮、熟紅蘿蔔、大黃瓜葉
片、熟芹菜梗、小花。

蘭花：熟蝦、大黃瓜葉片、熟菜梗、小花。

牡丹：馬鈴薯、熟蝦、南瓜、沙拉醬、青菜
葉、熟四季豆、熟紅蘿蔔。

梅花：熟茄子、香蕉、芥末醬、小花。

Food and Art

The color, smell, texture, taste, and shape
of a dish closely relate to art. The plea-
sure and importance of dining is empha-
sized by good food, a refined taste, and
proper timing which leads to good health.
By blending the skill of drawing into
Chinese cooking, delicate and beautiful
garnishes can be carved and arranged
together to present food and design
together as an appetizing art form.

Garnishes made from different kinds of
cooked foods, fruits, and vegetables,
beautifully work together to present food
as art on plates. These garnishes are
chrysanthemums, orchids, peony and
plum blossoms.

Ingredients:

Chrysanthemum: Chinese black mushroom, orange peel, cooked carrot,
cucumber (for the leaves), cooked celery
stalks, and small flowers.

Orchid: Cooked shrimp, cucumber (for
the leaves), any cooked stalk-shaped
vegetable, and small flowers.

Peony: Mashed potato, cooked shrimp,
squash, mayonnaise, green vegetable
leaves, cooked green beans and carrots.

Plum blossom: Cooked eggplant,
banana, mustard, and small flowers.

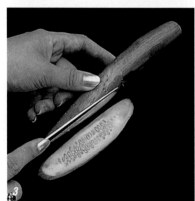

蘭花

1 蝦煮熟去頭除殼直切半，以剪刀分別剪出大小不同的花瓣。

2 取大黃瓜皮削成花托。

3 小黃瓜斜切長薄片，作為蘭花葉用。

4 以尖刀修切出葉片，菜梗煮熟作枝幹，熟蝦擺上當花瓣，與小花同置鏡盤上即成。

Orchids

1 Cut off the shrimp heads and shell them. Cut each shrimp lengthwise in half then cut them into different sizes to use for the petals; set aside.

2 Cut the cucumber skin into receptacles for the orchids.

3 Hold gherkin cucumber vertically. Cut thin slices, at a slant, for leaves.

4 Use a sharp-pointed knife to trim the edges to form leaves. Use any cooked stalk-shaped vegetable for the stems and cooked shrimp for petals of the orchids. Arrange orchids and small flowers on a plate.

• This garnish may be used on an appetizer platter.

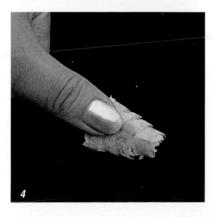

牡丹花

1 盤內放馬鈴薯泥；熟蝦8尾，剪出蝦頭及蝦尾後插入馬鈴薯泥中央作花心、花蕊。

2 12尾熟蝦，由蝦身處斜剪（帶殼），將蝦肉面向馬鈴薯處插入使尾巴向上揚，排一圈，再選較大的熟蝦，作法同上，但蝦的數量增多，以蝦尾向馬鈴薯泥插入，使蝦肉面向上揚，再排一圈。

3 最後取最大的熟蝦去頭尾，由腹部切一刀但不切斷備用。

4 將蝦身打開，以手指在蝦背上輕輕按一下使其張開（一端不按）作為牡丹花最外圍之花瓣，並插入馬鈴薯上，與南瓜盅（內放置沙拉醬）、青菜葉、熟四季豆及熟紅蘿蔔同置鏡盤上即成。

● 如有大型宴會可買大草蝦、明蝦或龍蝦以同樣方式來做，在色、香、味及視覺上的享受將更加完美。

Peony

1 Place a smooth mound of mashed potatoes on a plate, as shown. Cut off the heads and tails of eight cooked shrimp for the flower center.

2 Cut in half on a slant, twelve cooked shrimp. Insert the shrimp into the mashed potatoes, tail side up, and pointing toward the center, as petals of the second row. Use larger shrimp for the petals of the third row; follow the same procedures except insert the tails of the shrimp into the potatoes.

3 Cut off the heads and tails of large, cooked shrimp. Make a light cut on the belly of each shrimp, do not cut through.

4 Open each shrimp. Use a finger to gently press one end of the back, leaving other side intact. Insert shrimp into potatoes for the last layer of the peony. Place hollowed-out squash stuffed with mayonnaise, green vegetable leaves, cooked green beans and carrot beside the peony.

● For large banquets, shrimp may be substituted with prawns or lobsters.

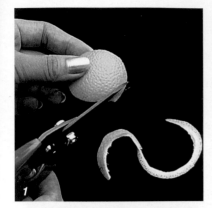

菊花

1 柳橙或香吉士皮，以剪刀修圓後，一端剪平做為花底。

2 以尖刀再片出一層薄皮，底部不片開。

3 平放檯上，以尖刀切細絲，底部不切斷。

4 展開即成菊花，香菇作法同，做好後與黃瓜葉片、熟菜梗及紅蘿蔔、小花同置鏡盤上擺飾即成。

Chrysanthemums

1 Use a large piece of orange peel; use scissors, cut a circular shape.

2 Use a sharp-pointed knife to cut between the skin and the pith, do not cut through to the other end.

3 Use the knife to shred the circular orange peel at open end; do not extend cut to the closed end.

4 Open the peel to form a chrysanthemum. Follow the same procedures to make Chinese black mushroom chrysanthemums. Place the leaves made from a cucumber, stalks from any cooked vegetable, carrot, and flowers appropriately to display chrysanthemums.

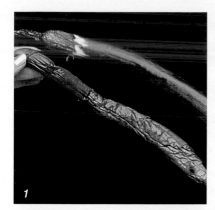

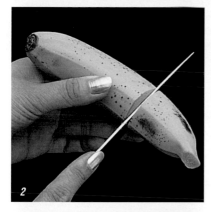

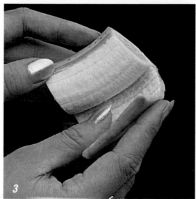

梅花

1 茄子燙熟至軟，將茄子皮帶肉直切，再分切出粗細不等的大小枝幹。

2 香蕉取一段。

3 去皮、並以香蕉自然之圓造型作花。

4 香蕉上挖5條直形溝，再切片成大朵的梅花（花心處擠上芥末醬），連同小花苞，分別擺在枝幹上，並與小花同置鏡盤上即可。

Plum Blossoms

1 Blanch a Chinese eggplant in boiling water until cooked. Cut the eggplant longthwise in half, then cut it into different sizes to form branches; set them aside.

2 Cut off a piece of banana.

3 Peel the piece of banana.

4 Vertically cut out 5 pieces around the banana to form scallops. Slice the banana into plum blossoms and calyxes. Arrange them on the plate. Put a small circular dab of mustard on the flower center, then arrange the branches and small flowers.

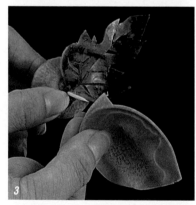

茶花

1 紅蘿蔔切三片圓薄片，每片自圓心向外切開一缺口。

2 蒜頭去皮用刀片成花瓣。

3 牙籤插入葉片（葉片做法參考第114頁），再插入三片缺口相疊的紅蘿蔔片。

4 最後插上蒜頭花瓣，泡水使用。

Camellia

1 Cut three thin carrot slices. Make a cut on the slices, from the center to the edge; set them aside.

2 Remove the skin from a clove of garlic. Cut petals on the garlic.

3 Insert a toothpick into the leaves (see p. 114). Overlap the cut ends of a carrot slice, then insert the toothpick into the overlapping ends to hold the carrot in place. Insert the toothpick on the remaining 2 slices in the same manner.

4 Finally, insert the toothpick into the garlic to make a camellia. Soak the flower in water until ready for use.

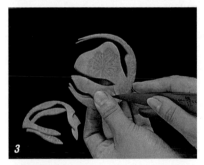

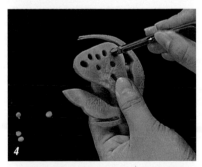

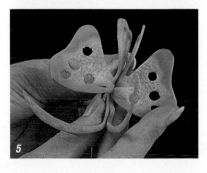

蝴蝶

1 大型紅蘿蔔修圓，切二開刀薄片，第一刀不切斷，第二刀切斷，使成一夾狀，相連處向下，此為蝶身，取尖刀由上往下先切出蝶鬚。

2 順著蝶鬚往下，續切出蝶身及蝶翼，剝除多餘的部份，使蝴蝶的造型現出。

3 在蝶身相連處直切一刀。

4 以圓雕刀及尖刀在蝶翼上挖圓，並做花紋。

5 翻開蝶翼，將蝶身缺口往前推即成，泡水後使用。

Butterfly

1 Trim a large carrot round. Cut double thin slices of carrot; do not cut through the first cut. Hold the double slices, connected edge down to serve as the body of the butterfly, cut antennas of the butterfly from the top to the bottom with a sharp-pointed knife.

2 Cut the shape of the wings and body. Remove excess carrot.

3 Make a cut on the connected edge of the butterfly's body, as shown.

4 Use a curved-blade carving tool and sharp-pointed knife to carve designs on the wings of the butterfly.

5 Open up the wings while holding the connected edge, separating the edge into two parts, done in step *3*. Lift the part with the antenna up and push back to rest it on the other part. Soak the butterfly in water before use.

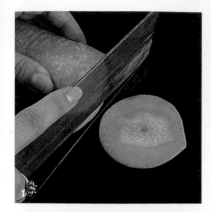

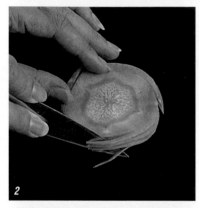

花

1 紅蘿蔔修圓切薄片，共切5片。

2 將薄片相疊置板上，以刀尖在邊緣等距共切出三條鬚（不切斷）。

3 取一片捲成花心，以牙籤穿上固定。

4 餘四片，每片對摺，再對摺，先在花心前後各插上一片，另取一片串上牙籤，由花心穿過後再插上另一片，（牙籤呈十字交叉），泡水後使用。

Flower

1 Trim a carrot to make it round. Cut five thin slices.

2 Stack the carrot slices. Lightly mark three points on the edge of the top slice with equal distance between points. Starting from one point, use the tip of a knife to cut close to the next point, leaving the strip joined; cut three strips of carrot.

3 Roll up one carrot slice for the flower center, secure it with a toothpick.

4 Carefully fold the other four carrot slices in half; fold them in half again. Skewer one folded slice with the toothpick and place it at the side of the flower center; repeat the same for other side. Insert another toothpick through the third folded slice then through the flower center and across the first toothpick. Put the last carrot slice on the toothpick on the fourth side of the flower center. Soak the flower in water until ready for use.

菊花魚鍋

1 牛肉、花枝、豬心、魚肉分別切薄片順序排好,中央處以金菇填滿,取剩餘材料切絲,圍成2個凹形墊座,以便擺入花。

2 蝦去殼由背部切一刀捲成環狀,鋪一圈在墊座上,花枝切長薄片,用手指勾成花瓣狀置於蝦上,並以櫻桃作花心,另一朵大花則先將花枝擺一圈。

3 再把蝦及櫻桃置其上。

4 以燙熟的芥菜梗作枝幹及葉片(參考第155頁),香菇當底,紅蘿蔔及大黃瓜片圍邊。

Chrysanthemums Platter

1 Cut beef, cuttlefish, pig's heart, and fillet into thin slices. Arrange the slices around a platter. Put golden mushroom in the center of the platter. Shred any leftover ingredients and arrange them into two mounds with concave centers.

2 Shell the shrimp. Make a cut on the back of each shrimp. Roll the shrimp into rings then arrange them around one of the mounds. Garnish with shredded carrot. Put cuttlefish rings on the shrimp. Use a cherry for the flower center to make a small chrysanthemum. Put large cuttlefish rings around the other mound.

3 Put a cherry and shrimp rings on the cuttlefish to make a large chrysanthemum.

4 Use blanched mustard green stalks for branches and leaves (see p. 155). Put presoaked and shredded Chinese black mushrooms at the bottom of the flowers. Arrange carrot and cucumber slices around the platter for garnishes.

• Ingredients on this platter are raw and cooked at the table when served.

菊花魚鍋

盤飾切花，講求的是刀工，尤其是切薄片，要注意切出的長寬、厚薄及間隔須一致，並依先後擺飾，才能顯得平衡有序，做花時要自然地摺疊，不能過份勉強，使作出的花飾呆板而不實際。

此拼盤所選用者多為生材料，適合一般火鍋類宴客，材料擺飾時須注意先後順序，才不致零亂，做法參考第121頁。

材料：牛肉、花枝、豬心、魚肉、金菇、蝦、紅蘿蔔、櫻桃、芥菜梗、香菇、大黃瓜。

Chrysanthemums Platter

The secret for a successful garnish flower is the cutting technique, especially when cutting thin slices. The size and thickness of the slices should be uniform and they should be arranged in cutting order. To give the flowers a natural look, fold the slices naturally; do not force them.

Most of the ingredients displayed on this platter are raw to be cooked at the table. Be careful to arrange the ingredients in cooking order. See page 121 for instructions on arranging the platter, which is suitable for banquets.

Ingredients:

Beef, cuttlefish, pig's heart, fillet, golden mushrooms, shrimp, carrot, cherries, mustard green stalk, Chinese black mushrooms, and cucumber.

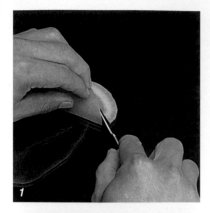

雙色花

1 紅蘿蔔直切開成二半，燙熟後，取半條斜切，第一刀不切斷，第二刀切斷。

2 攤開薄片，即成花片，共需5-6片。

3 將花片如圖擺飾成一朵花型。

4 小黃瓜片（切法同上）以鹽水泡軟，鋪在紅蘿蔔花片交錯間即成。

Two-colored Flower

1 Cut a carrot lengthwise in half, then boil it until cooked. Make a thin cut crosswise on the carrot; do not cut through. Make a second thin cut crosswise next to the first cut, slicing through the carrot to make a leaf. Follow the same procedure to make about four more leaves.

2 Open up the leaves.

3 Arrange the leaves to make a flower, as shown.

4 Follow the cutting procedure in step 1 to make cucumber leaves. Soak the cucumber in salty water until softened. Place the cucumber leaves in between the carrot leaves to arrange the flower petals.

三色花

1 漬黃蘿蔔直切半，取半條切片，第一刀不切斷，第二刀切斷，共需5組，每組攤開成花片。先將黃蘿蔔絲墊底，再將花片置其上，做為第一層花瓣。

2 紅蘿蔔直切半後燙熟，切法同上共切5組花片，與黃蘿蔔花片交錯鋪成第二層花瓣。

3 小黃瓜片（切法同上）以鹽水泡軟，交錯地鋪在紅蘿蔔花之間，做為第三層花瓣。

4 取碎黃蘿蔔作花蕊即成。

Three-colored Flower

1 Cut a takuruan (Japanese radish) lengthwise in half. Make a cut crossing the radish, do not cut through. Make a second cut crosswise above the first cut, cutting through the radish. Open it to make a leaf. Follow the same procedure to make four more leaves. Use a shredded takuruan as a base, put the leaves on the base as the first layer of the flower.

2 Cut a carrot lengthwise in half, then boil it until cooked. Follow the same procedure in step 1 to make the leaves. Put the carrot leaves in between the first layer, on the radish leaves, to make the second layer of the flower.

3 Follow the cutting procedure in step 1 to make cucumber leaves. Soak the cucumber in salty water until softened. Put the cucumber leaves in between the second layer, on the carrot leaves, to make the third layer of the flower.

4 Use chopped yellow radish for the flower center.

一枝獨秀

現今中國菜除了講求色、香、味外,更注重 "形" 的漂亮,形就是所謂的盤飾,搭配得宜 的盤飾,不僅上桌時讓人感覺賞心悅目,更能 引人入勝,想去品嚐。然而學習切雕不同於做 菜,除了平日要勤加練習外,更須具備創作藝 術品般的專注與投入的精神,才能運用智慧、 巧思,自創一格,使自己的技藝再提昇。

這一道宮保雞丁,以簡單的大黃瓜片、生菜、 巴西利及雞群(參考第129頁)裝飾,配上一 枝嫣紅的玫瑰(參考第128頁),清新的視覺 感受,不禁令人讚歎盤飾藝術的鬼斧神工。

To Outshine Others

Modern Chinese cooking not only empha-sizes color and smell of food, but also the appearance of the dish. Suitable garnish-es not only enhance the appearance of a dish by making it more appealing to the eye, but also create a craving to eat. Learning to make garnishes is different from learning to cook. Creating one's own style and improving carving skills demands continuous practice, concentra-tion, and devotion to this "art form". Effectively using one's own wisdom and thinking will enhance the creation. When garnishes are used for decoration, they should not take more than 1/4 of a plate so as not to usurp the appearance of the food. When preparing the garnish, keep the cuts clean so that the garnish will be neat and spotless.

Make the dish of "Chicken with Dried Red Chili Pepper" outstanding by using simple cucumber slices, lettuce, parsley, rooster (see p. 129), and a tree of roses (see p. 128), as garnishes.

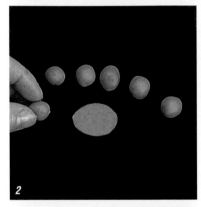

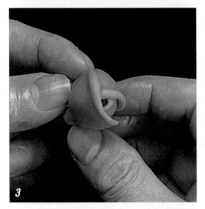

玫瑰

低筋麵粉1杯加滾水1/2杯及適量的糖先揉成麵糰後分二塊，分別加上紅、綠色素揉勻，醒約15分鐘備用。

1　綠色麵糰2小塊，搓成圓錐形，並以手掌按壓成葉子形，取尖刀先在葉片上畫葉脈，再以尖雕刀沿葉片邊緣做鋸齒紋。

2　捏一塊紅色麵糰，揉成7個小圓球，由小而大排列，先取最小的壓扁捲成花心，其餘6顆亦按壓做成6片花瓣（做時擦油，以免黏住）。

3　將3片較小花瓣圍繞在花心四周，包起第一層，使呈含苞狀。

4　餘3片則在第一層花瓣交錯間包起，使呈略開狀，如此即成一朵含苞待放的玫瑰，最後，將其放在2片做好的葉片中即可。

Rose

Mix together one cup of flour, 1/2 cup of boiling water and desired sugar. Knead into dough then cut in half. Color one half red and the other half green. Knead dough until smooth; let stand 15 minutes.

1　Cut two pieces of green dough; roll them into conical shapes. Lightly press the conical dough with the palm to make the leaves. Use a sharp-pointed knife to score veins on the leaves then cut V-shaped grooves around the edges of the leaves.

2　Cut off a piece of red dough; divide it into seven different size pieces. Grease the working board to prevent the dough from sticking to the board. Roll each piece of dough into a ball. Arrange the balls in order of size, from small to big. Lightly press the smallest ball to make the flower center. Press the other six balls with palm to make petals.

3　Arrange three small petals around the flower center to make the first petal layer.

4　Arrange the other three petals, alternating the petals between layers, around the first layer to make the rose. Put the leaves beside the rose.

公雞

1　備耐火土（建材行有售）。

2　耐火土加水調成有黏度的泥狀，取一塊捏圓作雞身，另一塊捏扁作出有弧度的尾巴黏上，以剪刀剪成鋸齒狀。

3　捏一雞頭黏上，邊黏邊沾水，將雞身全部抹勻。

4　黏上雞冠、肉垂，並以手或尖刀在嘴部略切一片，使嘴形突出。

5　尾部以尖雕刀畫長條，雞身以圓雕刀印出羽毛，分別塗上顏色即成。

●　亦可將雞肉塊依次包上荷葉、玻璃紙和耐火土後，捏成雞身，再按照作法 2 至 5 做成公雞，烤後即成土窯雞。

Rooster

1　Fire clay is available at building material centers.

2　Mix the fire clay with water to form a paste. Knead and form appropriate size pieces as needed. Knead a piece of the paste into the shape of the rooster's body. Knead and form another piece of the paste into the rooster's tail. Attach the tail to the body. Use scissors to cut V-shaped grooves at the end of the tail feathers.

3　Mold a piece of paste to form the rooster's head. Moisten the body of the rooster with water while attaching the head to the body.

4　Attach the comb and wattle to the rooster. With hand or sharp-pointed knife, cut a slit to form the beak.

5　Use sharp-pointed knife to score/carve feathers on the tail. Use curved-blade carving tool to carve feathers on the body of the rooster. Color the rooster as desired.

●　The fire clay rooster is used as garnish; however, it can also be used as a vessel for cooking. To make "Chicken Cooked in Fire Clay", wrap chicken pieces in lotus leaves, then wrap them together in plastic wrap. Use fire clay to form rooster around the wrapped chicken. Follow directions above to complete rooster, then bake until done.

水果大拼

取長形瓜身的西瓜,略切為船形後,挖除部份瓜肉作船身,上置各式水果,以瓜皮作帆,竹筷架起作船杆,取麻絲線綁緊即成一艘滿載的水果船,這種筵席式的水果大拼盤,只須將各式水果整個或稍切片擺上,不須刻意雕飾,顯得簡單又半實。

1 瓜皮切長10公分寬8公分,兩側內凹做帆。

2 以細竹在瓜皮上、下兩端距0.5公分處各串5個洞,並穿上麻絲線。

3 取竹筷(約11公分長)架在孔上,並綁上麻絲線(不綁死)。

4 另取一片穿好洞之瓜皮,連接第一片瓜皮,並打上死結固定,繼續作出6片中間主帆及前、後副帆各4片,再以長絲線串綁固定在主柱上使彼此間互相牽制,船帆插入船身時,才不會動搖。

● 作好的船身,可隨意擺上各種水果。同時在船外圍也可分別以切片的水果、果皮、巴西利、奶油擠花裝飾。

Assorted Fruit Platter

Cut a long shaped watermelon into a boat. Remove some of the melon for the hull. Use melon skin for the sails; wooden stick for the mast. Tie up the sails on the mast with string, as shown. Place different kinds of fruit on the boat. Arrange different kinds of fruit, whole or sliced, on the platter. No special arrangement is necessary. It is easy and practical.

1 Cut the melon into 4" X 3" (10cm X 8cm) pieces. Slightly bend both sides to make the sail.

2 At 1/4" (0.5cm) from the sail's edge, make 5 small holes on each side. Thread strings through the holes.

3 Use slip knots to tie the strings on a 4 1/2" (11cm) long stick.

4 To connect two pieces of melon, tie another piece of melon on the stick with fast knots. Use the same method to make six sails for the middle and four sails for each side. Secure the sails with string on the mast so that they will not slip when being put on the boat.

● Arrange desired fruit on the boat. Fruit slices, fruit skin, parsley may be used around outside of the boat for decoration.

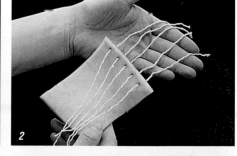

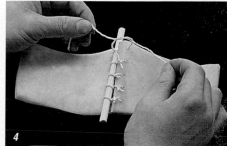

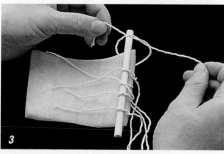

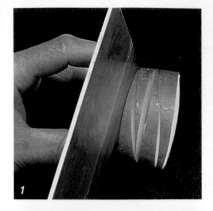

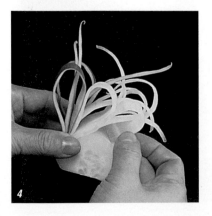

花（一）

1 大黃瓜取中段，先切去一塊當底座，以便可平放在盤上，在表皮切出一高一低的兩峰如Ｍ形，底端留1公分不要切到。

2 以刀片出薄皮，底端不切斷。

3 同法，再片出二層。

4 將一、二、三層的皮向內摺，使Ｍ二鬚上仰即成。

● 做好的黃瓜花須先泡水，使其展開。

Flowers I

1 Take a middle section of a cucumber, make two "V" cuts to 1/2" (1cm) from the bottom; make one point higher than the other to form an Ｍ shape.

2 Cut a thin, long continuous slice around and under the skin of the cucumber, leaving one end of skin intact and attached to the flesh.

3 Follow step **2** to make two more slices.

4 Tuck the ends of these slices in and make the pointed ends of Ｍ go up.

● Cucumber flower will open when soaked in water.

花（二）

1 取直切半的大黃瓜切片，第一刀不切斷，第二刀切斷，攤開備用。

2 黃瓜頭、尾段切出來的花瓣較小、中段切出來的花瓣較大，把大花瓣切去1/4即成中型花瓣，共需切出大中小三種不同的花瓣各5組。

3 取大花瓣先舖成花朵狀，在兩花瓣間放入中型花瓣，最後將小花瓣置上層，使呈一朵花型。

4 以碎紅蘿蔔當花蕊即成。

Flowers II

1 Cut a cucumber lengthwise in half. To make a petal: make a thin slice on the cucumber, do not cut through. Slice through a second cut. Open up the slices to make a petal. Continue cutting and slicing to make necessary petals.

2 Small petals are make from end section; large petals are make from middle section of a cucumber; medium petals are made by cutting off 1/4 of the large petals. Total petals needed are 5 for each size.

3 Arrange five large size petals for the first layer of the flower. Put medium size petals on top of the first layer, alternating the petals between layers. Put the smallest petals on top to make a flower.

4 Use chopped carrot for the flower center.

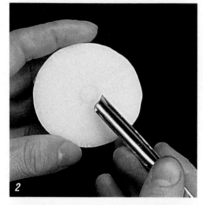

花（一）

1 取直切半的小黃瓜連續切9片，但一端要相連不切斷，輕拍成扇形葉片，共需2組。

2 白蘿蔔中段一塊，去皮，用中號圓雕刀在中心處刻一個小圓柱，頂部略修。

3 用中號尖雕刀沿著圓柱斜刻，並挖除5個花瓣型蘿蔔塊，續在同位置後方再斜刻一刀，此即第一層花瓣。

4 再以大號尖雕刀沿著第一層花瓣交錯間，同法雕出第二層大花瓣，如此刻出層層花瓣後，在花心及花瓣末端隨意染色，以增美觀。

Flower I

1 Cut a gherkin cucumber lengthwise in half. Diagonally cut nine slices on the cucumber, leaving one end attached. Follow the same procedure and make a second set of attached slices. Lightly press the slices open to make fans.

2 Pare a middle section of a daikon. Use curved-blade carving tool, medium size, to carve around daikon's center to form a short post.

3 Use a sharp-pointed knife to remove excess daikon around the post. Use a v-shaped-blade carving tool, medium size, to carve the first row of petals around the post. Remove excess daikon.

4 Continue the same way to carve the second row of petals with a large sized v-shaped-blade carving tool, alternating petals between the rows. Continve carving several rows until the flower is formed.

• Flower center and the edge of petals may be colored to highlight petals.

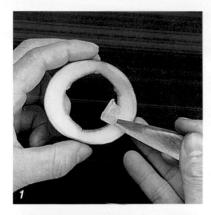

花（二）

1 大黃瓜中段切1公分厚，挖除瓜肉當底座。

2 另切出中段及尾段各1塊，成一大一小，對切成半圓形切口向下，在瓜皮上切出直條紋，再切薄片，第一刀不切斷，第二刀切斷，大小各切5組，每組一端切去1/3後，攤開成大小葉片，並將大葉片先插入底座，續插小葉片。

3 白蘿蔔中段去皮，修成圓筒狀，旋轉片出長條薄片，對摺，在摺起的一端切絲狀，底端留1公分不切斷（間隔愈密，花瓣愈細），切好後捲起成花朵，底部以牙籤固定，並在花蕊處染色。

4 染好的白蘿蔔花，放入鋪好葉片的底座中即成。

Flower II

1 Cut a middle section of a cucumber, 1/2" (1cm) thick. Hollow out the flesh of the cucumber to make a flower holder (base).

2 To make the leaves, cut a middle section and an end section of a cucumber. Cut both sections lengthwise in half. Cut straight lines down the length of the skin of both sections. To make individual leaves, cut two thin slices on cucumber sections, do not cut through the first cut; leave the two slices intact. Open up the slice to reveal a leaf. Make five larger leaves from the middle section and five smaller leaves from the end section. Put the large leaves on the holder for the first layer of the flower. Put the small leaves on top of the first layer, alternating the leaves between layers.

3 Pare a middle section of a daikon. Trim the daikon into a cylindrical shape. Hold the cutting knife parallel to the daikon; peel off a long, thin, continuous slice. Fold the slice in half lengthwise. Cut narrow strips across the fold, slice to 1/2" (1cm) from the long, open edges. To make a flower more dense and more beautiful, cut narrower strips for more layers. Take one end of the folded daikon strips and roll up like a jelly roll. Secure the ends with a toothpick; then spread. Color the top of the flower.

4 Put the flower on top of the leaves.

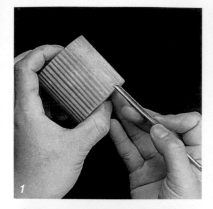

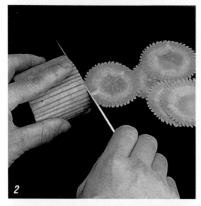

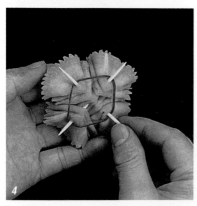

康乃馨

1 紅蘿蔔去皮，取中段，以尖雕刀雕直線條。

2 切薄片，共切9片。

3 取一片對摺2次，以牙籤插入，同法續插入4片，注意一片朝左一片朝右，呈不規則狀，另取牙籤由中央處穿過呈十字形交叉，左右兩邊亦各插上2片，即成一朵康乃馨。

4 在背面牙籤交叉處，以橡皮筋扣上固定，泡水使用。

Carnation

1 Use a V-shaped-blade carving tool to cut vertical grooves around the length of the middle section of a pared carrot.

2 Cut nine thin slices from the carrot.

3 Fold each slice in fourths. Rotate a toothpick while inserting it into five folded slices, alternate the slices by placing the folded side of one slice toward left and the next slice toward right. Insert another toothpick crosswise through the center. Skewer two slices on both sides of the second toothpick.

4 Use a rubber band to secure the slices on the toothpicks.

• To open up the petals, soak the carnation in water.

花（一）

1　紅蘿蔔去皮切長7公分，寬2公分的長方形薄片，以鹽水（鹽1/2大匙加水1杯）泡軟，取一片對角處先對摺。

2　捲成花心。

3　第一層以3片對摺之花瓣圍繞花心，第二層起花瓣慢慢增加，花朵的大小可隨意，只要花瓣交錯不重疊即可。

4　做好後，另取一紅蘿蔔薄片，圈住底部，使花瓣不致鬆掉，放入底座（參考第135頁）即成。

●　材料除紅蘿蔔外，亦可以蘋果、白蘿蔔、漬黃蘿蔔、香菇、花枝、腰片、火腿等代替。

Flower I

1　Pare a carrot then cut it into 2 3/4" x 3/4" (7cm x 2cm) slices. Soak the slices in a salt solution of 1/2 tablespoon salt dissolved in 1 cup of water until soft. Diagonally fold a slice in half.

2　Roll up the slice to make the flower center.

3　Diagonally fold three slices in half, put the slices around the flower center for the petals of the first row. Follow the same procedures to make several rows, alternating between the rows. Do not overlap the petals. Adjust the size of the flower as desired.

4　Secure the flower by wrapping one or two carrot slices, depending on the size of the flower, around the lower part of the flower. Put the flower in a flower holder (see p. 135).

●　A presoaked apple in salt solution, takuruan, daikon, Chinese black mushroom, cuttlefish, kidney, or ham may be used to substitute for carrot.

蘋果盤飾 · APPLE GARNISH

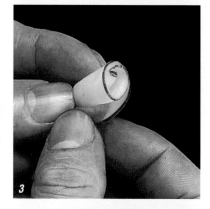

花（二）

1 蘋果半個切薄片，泡鹽水使變軟。

2 青江菜燙熟，取梗部斜切薄片，第一刀不切斷，第二刀切斷，攤開成葉片，置於底座上（參考第135頁）。

3 將蘋果片一片片捲成花苞。

4 捲好的花苞放入舖好葉片的底座中，花心處以少許紅蘿蔔絲點綴。

Flower II

1 Cut an apple in half. Cut the apple into thin semi-circle slices. Soak the slices in water to soften.

2 Use the stalk of a cooked bok choy for the leaves. Make a diagonal cut on the stalk, do not cut through. Make a second diagonal cut above the first cut, cutting through the stalk. Open it up to make a leaf. Arrange leaves around rim of a cucumber (flower seat, see step *1* of p. 135).

3 Roll each apple slice horizontally to make flower buds.

4 Arrange the buds on the leaves. Decorate the center of the buds with shredded carrot.

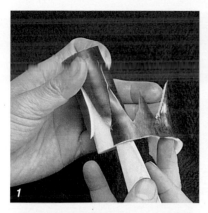

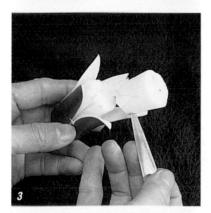

花

1 茄子一段以尖刀在表皮切5片細長花瓣，並沿花瓣周圍切除多餘的茄子皮。

2 取尖刀順著花瓣片出薄片。

3 切斷中央1/2的茄肉，並修圓。

4 續用尖刀在五角柱處切出5片花瓣，與第一圈花瓣交錯，去除多餘的茄肉及茄心，使花朵突顯出來。

● 亦可任意在茄皮畫上自己喜愛的花紋。

Flower

1 Use a sharp-pointed knife to cut five long, pointed petals on a section of a Chinese eggplant. Cut around the length of the eggplant to remove the excess skin.

2 Use the knife to cut along the petals to separate the skin from the flesh.

3 Horizontally, cut off half of the center flesh. Trim to round the center flesh.

4 Use the knife to cut five petals of the second row on the white flesh, alternating the petals between rows. Remove excess eggplant to complete the flower.

● A picture may be carved on the skin of the eggplant.

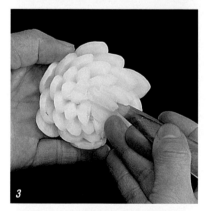

花

1 洋蔥半個，以尖刀在表面切出6片尖或橢圓形花瓣（深度不超過1層洋蔥），並取出花瓣間多餘的洋蔥。

2 在第一層花瓣交錯間，續切第二層花瓣，去除多餘部份。

3 依照上面作法層層切出花瓣，但愈往裡層，花瓣愈少。

4 用巴西利或其他葉片沾染料，在花心處染色，放入清水內，稍以手撥動，使色澤均勻。

Flower

1 Horizontally, cut an onion in half. Use a sharp-pointed knife to cut six pointed or oval petals on the onion, as shown; do not cut deeper than one layer. Remove excess onion between the petals.

2 Cut the second row of petals, alternating petals between rows. Remove excess onion between the petals.

3 Follow step **2** to cut more rows of petals. Reduce number of petals in each row when cutting toward center.

4 Dip some parsley or other leaves in coloring then dab the color on the flower center with the leaves. Put the flower in water then stir the water to distribute the color evenly.

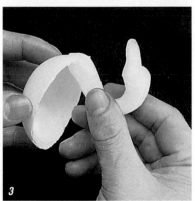

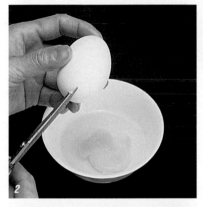

天鵝

1 白蘿蔔一片以尖刀在上端中央處斜刀切出一 V 形缺口當嘴，再左右各切除二大塊，修出鵝頭及頸部，將做好的鵝頭略修飾圓滑。

2 雞蛋殼剪半，一半做鵝身，另一半再剪半後成二片翅膀（剪時力道偏左，可保持右半邊的蛋殼完整，不碎裂）。

3 白蘿蔔做的鵝頭在頸部下方切一刀，插入蛋殼鵝身，使成為一隻天鵝。

4 鵝身內裝入少許生米，使其有重量，不致傾斜，並在左右兩側裝上翅膀即成。

● 由於生米色略黃，故可在上層再蓋上少許白細砂糖，以求色澤美觀。

Swan

1 Pare a daikon. Diagonally cut a middle section of the daikon into ⌒ shape. Cut off a small wedge from the top center to form the beak. Cut off two larger wedges from both sides. Trim to form the head and the neck of the swan then slice it. Trim the swan's head round.

2 Slightly left from the center of one end of an egg, use a V-shaped carving tool to carefully pierce a hole. Pour out the egg yolk and egg white through the hole. Starting from the hole, insert a small scissors and slant them slightly left, cut the egg shell lengthwise in half. Keeping the scissors slightly left when cutting can prevent the right side of the shell from breaking. Use the right half shell for the body of the swan. Cut the other half shell into two wings.

3 Make a slit on the bottom of the swan's neck to insert it into the body of the swan.

4 Put some rice into the body of the swan to give weight to keep the swan still. Put the wings on both sides of the swan's body.

● Powdered sugar may be sprinkled on the rice for whiteness.

鳳凰于飛

鳳凰是古時候傳說的瑞鳥，以紅蘿蔔雕飾一幅
鳳求凰的景象，再配上各種花草點綴，在婚宴
時最能表達美滿姻緣，象徵百年好合。

做法參考第150、151頁。

Phoenixes

The phoenix is an auspicious bird revered
in China's ancient legends. Carrots are
carved into two phoenixes on the wing to
show a scene of courtship representing a
future happy marriage. Decorate the
phoenixes with flowers and grass. This
garnish is most suitable for a wedding,
providing a special congratulatory mes-
sage of a harmonious union lasting a hun-
dred years.

To make a phoenix, see pp. 150, 151.

你儂我儂

初學者持刀要盡量以鋸的方式較易切出圖形輪廓，不致斷裂，學習切雕貴在有恆，並非一蹴可及，讀者們要多看、多做，才能領會其中的奧妙，創造出更好的傑作。

此種盤飾須使用較大的白蘿蔔或芋頭來做，瞧！一對對昂首或低頭依偎呢噥的天鵝，叫人好生羨慕。

做法參考第148、149頁。

Courting Swans

It is easier for beginners to cut the outline of a picture, without breaking the material, by using a sawing motion. It takes time and lasting effort to learn the cutting technique. Readers should observe and effectively practice repeatedly to understand the secret of cutting to create unique centerpieces.

Use large daikon or taro for this garnish. Some swans hold their heads high and some lower their heads as if courting each other.

To make a swan, see pp. 148, 149.

做好的菜餚配上白天鵝（參考第148頁）及芥菜花（參考第155頁），顯得精緻、美觀。

Garnishing the dish with mustard green flowers (p. 155) and a swan (p. 148) adds beauty and delicacy to the dish.

白色菜餚以簡單的生菜、小黃瓜片、櫻桃及紅蘿蔔來點綴；紅、綠相間，不僅高雅而且清爽。

Garnish white food with simple lettuce, gherkin cucumber slices, cherries, and carrot; red and green colors make the dish look elegant and refreshing.

小黃瓜斜切片，一邊不切斷，稍拍使其張開略成扇形，左右二片對稱，中央配上蛋及櫻桃，恰似一隻隻彩蝶活躍在餐盤上。

Diagonally cut a gherkin cucumber into several slices, leaving one end intact. Lightly press the slices to spread like a fan. Place half an egg and cherry between two fans to make a butterfly. Garnish the dish with several butterflies.

以紅蘿蔔片、茄子片及大黃瓜片排列而成的方形盤飾，簡單又不失高雅。

Arrange slices of carrot, eggplant, and cucumber to make a square garnish. It is easy and elegant.

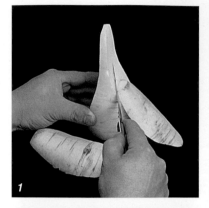

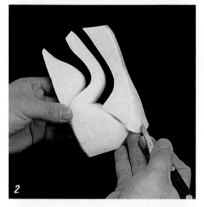

天鵝（一）

1 白蘿蔔切除左右二片，上端留寬約1公分。

2 將切面朝前，刻劃出鵝的形狀。

3 修飾鵝身使輪廓圓滑，並做出底座，在鵝背兩旁切出二條溝痕。二片白蘿蔔切出翅膀，再切鋸齒紋，裝在切出的二條溝內。

4 取火柴棒插入當眼睛，嘴部套上紅辣椒即成。

Swan I

1 Cut off two pieces on both sides of a daikon, leaving the top about 1/2" (1cm) wide.

2 Holding cut side of daikon toward you, cut out a swan's shape.

3 Trim the body of the swan. Cut the bottom stand. Cut two slits on the back of the swan for inserting the wings. Use the point of a knife to cut the shape of the wings on two daikon slices. Cut grooves on the trailing edges of the wings. Insert the wings into the swan.

4 Insert matchsticks for eyes and a red chili pepper for the swan's beak.

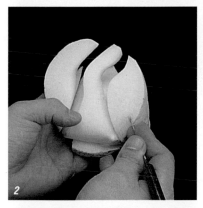

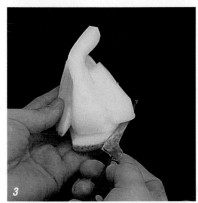

天鵝（二）

1　白蘿蔔一段左面傾斜45°切除一片如 ▭，右面斜切二刀至中心處交接，去除三角塊，使呈 ᘓ 形。

2　將第一刀斜切面朝前，續切除左右二塊，刻劃鵝身輪廓。

3　修飾鵝身並做出底座，再切出左右翅膀及尾部，並加以修飾使其線條分明。

4　在翅膀兩旁以圓雕刀雕出羽毛狀花紋，翅尾則以尖刀劃出，同時將底座修成鋸齒紋，最後插入火柴棒當眼睛，套上紅辣椒當嘴巴。

Swan II

1　Cut at a 45° angle, and remove a piece from a section of a daikon, i.e. ▭. Make two slant cuts to the center of the daikon to remove a wedge to form the following shape of ᘓ.

2　While holding cut side of the daikon toward you, cut off one piece on each side then cut the shape of the swan's body.

3　Trim the body of the swan. Cut the bottom as a base. Cut the shape of the wings and tail of the swan then trim them.

4　Use curved-blade carving tool to carve feathers on the wings. Carve the tail of the swan with a sharp-pointed knife. Cut grooves on the base. Insert matchsticks for the eyes and a red chili pepper for the beak of the swan.

鳳凰

1 紅蘿蔔斜切除左右二片成錐形。

2 由上端開始以鋸的方式依續切出鳳的嘴形、肉垂、頸部和頭形。

3 續切前胸及後背。

4 鳳身處以圓雕刀雕羽毛，下端切出鋸齒紋。同時在背部切出四條溝痕以備裝大、小翅膀。

5 紅蘿蔔片先切出翅膀的形狀，再以尖形雕刀刻劃直條紋，作出二對大小不同的鳳翅。

6 另外切出一對中間鳳尾，一對左右鳳尾及三片尾部鳳尾（一片較小）。

7 在鳳身底部切2條4公分×1公分之凹槽（備裝中間鳳尾），並在凹槽之上端切三條深溝，左右再各切出一條深溝（備裝尾部鳳尾及左右鳳尾），如 ▐▐ 。

8 將中間鳳尾插入鳳身底部之凹槽內，三片尾部鳳尾裝在凹槽上方之深溝（較小的一片在上），再裝上左右鳳尾，即完成鳳身底部之動作。

9 將做好的二對大小翅膀插於鳳身背部之深溝內，以火柴頭套上當鳳眼。

10 如意鳳冠，套上牙籤置頭頂上方即成。

Phoenix

1 Diagonally cut off two pieces on opposite sides of carrot, to form a conical shape carrot.

2 From the top of the carrot, use a sawing motion to cut the shape of phoenix's beak, wattle, neck, and head.

3 Cut the shape of the breast and back of the phoenix.

4 Use a curved-blade carving tool to carve the feathers on the body; cut grooves on the end of the body, cut two large slits and two small slits on the back of the phoenix for inserting the wings.

5 Make two large wings and two small wings, using the tip of a sharp-pointed knife to cut the shape of the wings on carrot slices. Carve straight lines on the wings by using a v-shaped-blade carving tool.

6 On carrot slices, cut a pair of tails for the center, a pair of tails for both sides, and three tails for the top (one tail is smaller than the other two).

7 Cut two grooves, 1 1/2" x 1/2" (4cm x 1cm), on the bottom of the body of the phoenix for inserting the center tails; cut three slits above and one slit for each side of the grooves for inserting the other tails, as shown ▮▮ .

8 Insert the two center tails into the grooves, three tails in the three slits above the grooves (the smaller one on top in the upper slit), and two tails in both side slits.

9 Insert two large wings and two small wings in the slits on the back of the phoenix. Insert matchsticks for the eyes.

10 Cut a carrot slice the shape of a comb and affix it to the head of the phoenix with a toothpick.

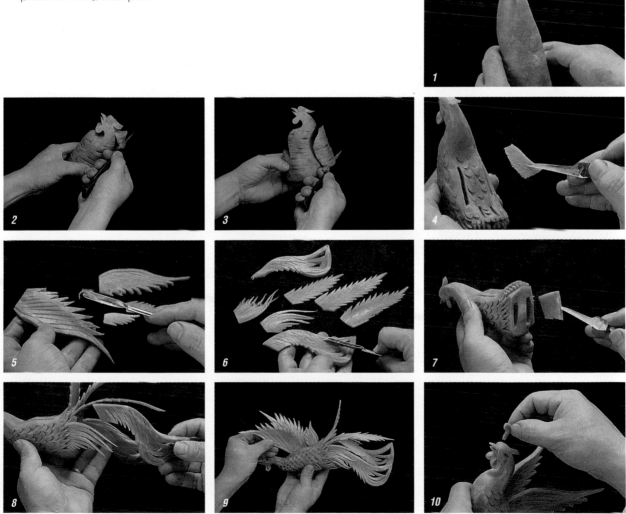

龍

1 紅蘿蔔去皮切 ⌐‾¯ 形，先在右上角切去一小塊作上嘴唇，如 ⌐‾¯■。

2 斜切除一三角塊如 ⌐‾▼，並在突起的蘿蔔塊中央分切出一對龍角如 ⌐ᴹᴹ。

3 在斜三角塊上續切出鼻形及嘴形，加以修飾，使輪廓現出。

4 切出舌頭及下巴，並將牙齒及齒痕作出。

5 龍頭做好後，左右兩側修切出腮狀。

6 緊接著腮後，在頸部續切出二薄片修成鬚狀，並以尖刀在嘴部四周修出鋸齒紋，用圓雕刀在龍身四周雕出麟片狀花紋，最後取芋頭修圓套入火柴頭作眼睛，紅蘿蔔切2條捲曲的細長條作龍鬚，前端修圓，在鼻子兩旁挖洞，裝上即成。

● 做好的龍身可挖成凹形，用來盛放各種沾料。

Dragon

1 Pare a carrot. Cut a carrot into the following shape ⌐‾¯. Cut off a small piece on the right upper corner, as ⌐‾¯■, for upper lip of the dragon.

2 Cut off a triangle wedge, as shown ⌐‾▼. Cut a pair of horns on the center raised portion of the daikon, as shown ⌐ᴹᴹ. Remove excess daikon.

3 Cut the shape of the dragon's nose and mouth on the triangle of the daikon. Remove a piece from the mouth then trim it to make the mouth stand out.

4 Cut the shape of the dragon's tongue, chin, and teeth.

5 Cut the shape of the dragon's ears, remove excess daikon to emphasize the ears.

6 Cut two thin, intacted slices behind each ear, then cut grooves on the edge of the slices. Insert toothpicks into two pieces of trimmed taro root for the eyes of the dragon. Use a curved-blade carving tool to cut decorative designs on both sides of the dragon's body. Use a sharp-pointed knife to cut grooves around the mouth and the neck. Cut two curved strips of carrot for the antenna of the dragon. Make a slit on each side of the nose then insert the carrot strips in the slits.

● Dragon's body may be hollowed out and used to serve dipping sauce, as shown.

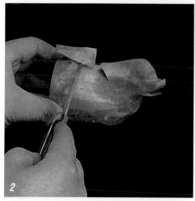

鴛鴦

1. 紅蘿蔔去頭尾，先由一端切除左右二塊使中央突起。再雕出鴛鴦的輪廓、嘴部及下巴。

2. 將輪廓修飾完整，並在頭部後方斜切一塊，使頭形現出。

3. 在背部左右兩旁切劃出翅膀，身後處並切出有弧度的尾巴，再將整隻鴛鴦修飾圓滑。

4. 切除尾部下方多餘的蘿蔔，取尖雕刀在頭部、背部、尾部及翅膀後端刻劃直條紋，翅膀前則以圓雕刀雕出羽毛狀花紋，下端小翅部份則用尖刀切成羽尾，套上火柴棒當眼睛即成。

Mandarin Duck

1. Cut off both ends of a carrot. Cut off two pieces on one end of the carrot to form a raised center. Cut the shape of the duck. Cut the shape of the bill and the chin.

2. Cut off a piece behind the head to show the shape of the head.

3. Cut the shape of the wings and the tail. Trim the duck.

4. Remove excess carrot under the tail of the duck. Use a V-shaped blade carving tool to cut a straight line on the head, back, tail, and one end of the wings. Use a curved-blade carving tool to carve feathers on the other end of the wings. Cut small wings under the large wings with a sharp-pointed knife. Insert matchstick ends for the eyes of the duck.

圍邊盤飾 · GARNISHES AROUND THE PLATE

在日常生活中，隨手就能做出這四款漂亮又大方的盤飾，這些均取材於切片的果、蔬及果皮，只要稍微注意配色，就可以了。

盤飾 1
材料：茄子、紅蘿蔔、小黃瓜、柳丁

盤飾 2
材料：柳丁皮、番茄、紅蘿蔔、大黃瓜

盤飾 3
材料：柳丁、大黃瓜、紅蘿蔔、櫻桃

盤飾 4
材料：茄子、紅蘿蔔、小黃瓜、櫻桃

Slices of fruit, vegetables, and fruit skin can be easily arranged into the following four beautiful garnishes. These simple and beautiful garnishes may be adapted for daily use by choosing desired color and ingredients.

Garnish 1
Ingredients: Slices of eggplant, carrot, gherkin cucumber and orange.

Garnish 2
Ingredients: Wedges of orange peel, tomato, carrot and cucumber.

Garnish 3
Ingredients: Cherries, Slices of orange, cucumber and carrot.

Garnish 4
Ingredients: Cherries, slices of eggplant, carrot and gherkin cucumber.

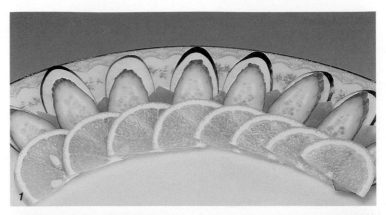

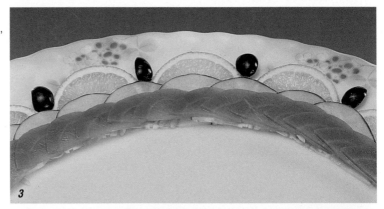

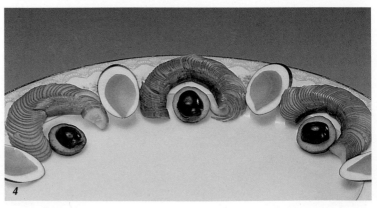

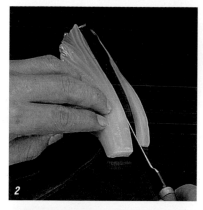

花

1 芥菜1棵洗淨備用。

2 入滾水中燙熟，切去葉片，取梗部，直放切細條作枝幹。

3 另取燙熟的梗部，斜切薄片，第一刀不切斷，第二刀切斷，攤開成葉片。

4 將枝幹、葉片分別擺好，並以櫻桃當果實裝飾。

Flower

1 Wash the mustard greens.

2 Blanch them in boiling water. Cut off the leaves. Cut the center stalk lengthwise to make long strips for the branches.

3 Cut off a piece from the side of the stalk to make a leaf. Make a diagonal cut, do not cut through. Make a second diagonal cut above the first cut, cutting through the stalk. Open the leaf.

4 Arrange the branches and leaves as desired. Cherries may be used for flower buds.

"觀音" - 呂瑞義 "Goddess of Mercy" by Jui-I Lu

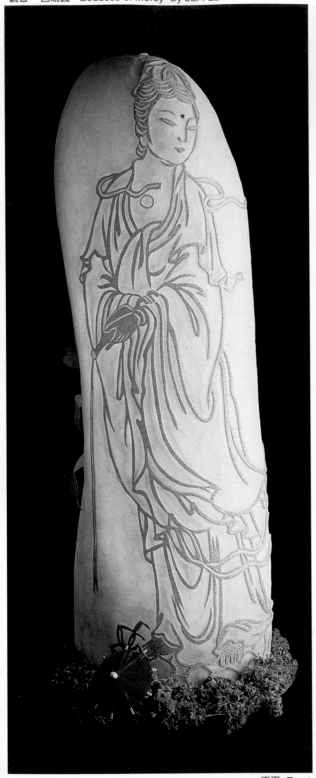

正面 Front

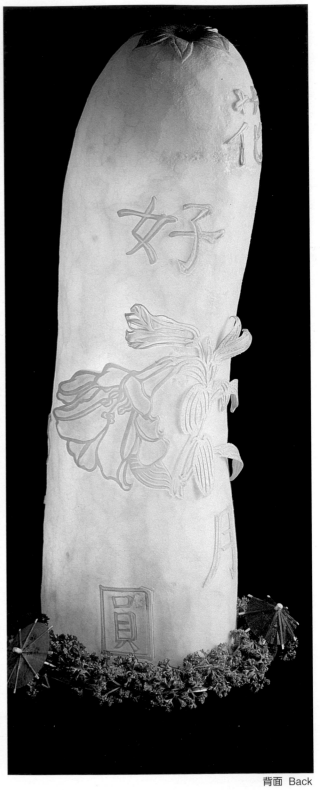

背面 Back

"切雕小品" - 陳兆麟
"Little Treasures" by Choa Lin Chen

"馬騰雲山" - 魏幸助 "Galloping Horses" by Shin-Chu Wei

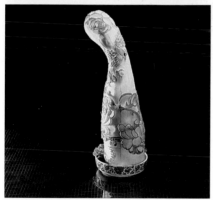

觀音、切雕小品、馬騰雲山

冬瓜1條，先以鉛字筆在瓜皮描繪圖形，再以雕花刀刻出線條，並削去多餘的瓜皮（厚約0.4公分），使輪廓現出。挖除瓜籽及部份瓜肉，瓜肉留約2公分厚，備裝日光燈管。（瓜肉太厚不透明，太薄則亦反射），做好的冬瓜盤飾以濕布覆蓋（須天天換布保濕）可保存5天，若放入冰箱冷藏則可保存10天。

除冬瓜外，亦可取材南瓜或西瓜，惟西瓜水份多，購回宜置放2～3天至蒂頭乾、水份少時再做，較不易斷裂。

此種盤飾藉著燈光的烘托，顯得豪華而別緻，喜慶或壽宴時可雕些駿馬、龍鳳、鴛鴦、松鶴、壽桃及其他小品等配合用場裝飾。

Goddess of Mercy · Little Treasures · Galloping Horses

Cut the desired length of a don quia (pale squash). Draw a design on the don quia (pale squash) with a marker. Carve the lines with carving tools. Remove excess skin, 1/8" (0.3cm) thick, to reveal the design. Hollow out the seeds and the flesh of the don quia (pale squash) to accommodate the fluorescent light. For the best results, leave 3/4" (2cm) thick flesh with the skin. The garnishes may be kept for ten days if they are covered with a wet cloth, changing daily to keep them wet, and refrigerated.

Pumpkin or watermelon may be used for this garnish. If watermelon is used, let it stand for 2 or 3 days after purchase to reduce the juice and to prevent it from breaking.

It will look luxurious and fresh when the light is on. Horses, dragons, phoenix, mandarin duck, pine tree and crane, longevity peaches, etc., may be carved on the don quia (pale squash) for other suitable banquets or celebrations.

索 引

INDEX

Wei-Chuan Cookbooks can be purchased in the U.S.A., Canada and twenty other countries worldwide
1455 Monterey Pass Road, #110, Monterey Park, CA 91754, U.S.A. • Tel: (323)261-3880 • Fax: (323) 261-3299
E-Mail: wc@weichuancookbook.com • Website: www.weichuancookbook.com

國立中央圖書館出版品預行編目資料

盤飾精選＝Great garnishes／黃淑惠作，——
初版．—〔臺北市〕：味全，民81印刷
面：　公分
ISBN 957-9285-07-1（精裝），— ISBN 957-
9285-08-X（平裝）

　　1.蔬果雕切

427.3　　　　　　　　　　　　81001393